TUNES, TALES, & TRUTHS

PAM & STAN CAMPBELL

TUNES, TALES, & TRUTHS

A DIVISION OF SCRIPTURE PRESS PUBLICATIONS INC.
USA CANADA ENGLAND

BibleLog Thru the Old Testament Series
Book 1   Let There Be Life (Genesis thru Ruth)
Book 2   Who's Running This Kingdom? (1 Samuel thru 2 Chronicles)
Book 3   Tunes, Tales, and Truths (Ezra thru Song of Songs)
Book 4   Watchmen Who Wouldn't Quit (Isaiah thru Malachi)

BibleLog Thru the New Testament Series
Book 1   When God Left Footprints (Matthew thru John)
Book 2   Good News to Go (Acts thru 1 Corinthians)
Book 3   Priority Mail (2 Corinthians thru Philemon)
Book 4   Home At Last (Hebrews thru Revelation)

BibleLog for Adults is an inductive Bible study series designed to take you through the Bible in 2 years if you study one session each week. This eight-book series correlates with SonPower's **BibleLog** series for youth. You may want to use **BibleLog** in your daily quiet time, completing a chapter a week by working through a few pages each day. Or you may want to use this series (along with the SonPower **BibleLog** series) in family devotions with your teenagers. This book also includes a leader's guide for use in small groups.

Scripture taken from the *Holy Bible, New International Version* ®. Copyright © 1973, 1978, 1984 by International Bible Society. Used by permission of Zondervan Publishing House. All rights reserved.

Designer: Joe DeLeon
Cover Illustration: Jeff Nishinaka
Interior Illustrations: Arnie Ten

Library of Congress Catalog Card Number: 92-82618
ISBN: 0-89693-873-5

Recommended Dewey Decimal Classification: 221
Suggested Subject Heading: BIBLE STUDY: OLD TESTAMENT

1 2 3 4 5 6 7 8 9 10 Printing/Year 96   95 94 93 92

© 1992, SP Publications, Inc.
All rights reserved.
Printed in the United States of America.

CONTENTS

BEFORE YOU BEGIN..6
FROM THE AUTHORS...9
  1. The Fifth-Century B.C. Homecoming Parade 11
  2. When the Walls Came Tumblin' Up 23
  3. What a Coincidence! 35
  4. What Did I Do to Deserve This!? 47
  5. Straight from the Source's Mouth 59
  6. Intro to Old Testament Lit 71
  7. Honest to God 81
  8. Jerusalem Bandstand 93
  9. Are You a Wise Guy or Just a Smart Aleck? 107
  10. The Wise Have It 119
  11. Satisfaction Isn't Guaranteed 135
  12. Just an Old-Fashioned Love Song 145
BEFORE YOU LEAVE..155

LEADER'S GUIDE 157
Session 1 159
Session 2 160
Session 3 161
You're in Control, Lord 162
Session 4 163
Session 5 165
Session 6 166
Session 7 168
Session 8 169
Session 9 171
Session 10 172
Session 11 174
Session 12 175
Review 177

WRAP-UP...179

BEFORE YOU BEGIN

Welcome to Book 3 in the
BibleLog Thru the Old Testament Series

Though the Bible continues to be one of the world's best-selling books, few people are familiar enough with it to comprehend "the big picture." They may know many of the specific stories about Abraham, Samson, Jonah, Jesus, Peter, Paul, and so forth. Yet most people are unsure how these characters fit into the broad historic groupings—patriarchs, judges, kings, prophets, Gospels, epistles, etc.

That's why we are introducing the **BibleLog Thru the Old Testament Series.** The purpose of the **BibleLog** studies is to guide you through the Old Testament in one year, at the rate of one session per week. This series eliminates the perceived drudgery of Bible reading by removing unnecessary references and explaining the material in clear terms that anyone can understand. The pace should be fast enough to propel you through the material without getting bogged down, yet slow enough to allow you to see things you never noticed before. First-time readers will feel completely at ease as they explore the Bible on their own. Yet no matter how many times the person has been through the Bible, this study will provide fresh insight.

WHAT MAKES BIBLELOG DIFFERENT?

Countless thousands of adults have, at some point in their lives, decided to read through the Bible. Pastors, Sunday School teachers, Bible study leaders, or peers have preached the benefits of "Read your Bible," "Get into the Word," "Meditate on Scripture," and so forth. And after hearing so many worthwhile challenges, a lot of determined, committed adults have dusted off the covers of their Bibles and set themselves to the task ahead.

They usually make a noble effort too. The first couple of Bible books whiz past before they know it. The next few books aren't quite as fast-paced, but they have their strong points. Then comes a tough passage. In most cases, the Gospels are enough to do in even the most eager readers. And instead of feeling like they've accomplished something, all those people feel is guilt because they didn't finish what they started.

That's why this Bible study series was developed. It calls for a one-year commitment on your part to get through the Old Testament. By following the session plans provided, you only need to complete one session each week to accomplish your one-year goal. You won't read the entire Old Testament word for word, but you will go much more in-depth than most of the Old Testament overviews you may have tried. You will still be challenged just to get through the major flow of Old Testament action in one year.

WHAT ARE THE FEATURES OF BIBLELOG?

- **THE WHOLE BIBLE** Not a verse-by-verse study, but an approach that hits all the books without skipping major passages.

- **THE RIGHT PACE** By completing one session each week (a couple of pages per day), you will get through the Old Testament in one year.

- **A FRESH APPROACH** The inductive design allows you to personally interact with biblical truth. Longer, drier passages are summarized in the text, and difficult passages are explained, but you are kept involved in the discovery process at all times.

- **INSTANT APPLICATION** Each weekly session concludes with a **Journey Inward** section of practical application that allows you to respond to the content immediately. The goal is to help you apply the truths of the Bible today.

- **GROUP STUDY OPTION** A leader's guide is included to promote discussion and further application if desired. After a week of self-study, a time of group interaction can be very effective in reinforcing God's truth. Each book covers 13 weeks.

- **REASONABLE PRICE** The entire set of 4 Old Testament **BibleLog** books costs no more than a basic Bible commentary. And after completing the series, you will have a self-written commentary of the Old Testament for future reference.

- **48 DIFFERENT TOPICS** Over a one-year period of study, you will be challenged to apply what the Bible has to say about 48 different topics, including God's sovereignty, murder, homosexuality, obedience, family relationships, and much more.

HOW CAN YOU GET THE MOST OUT OF BIBLELOG?

We recommend a group study for this series, if possible. If group members work through the content of the sessions individually during the week, the time your group needs to spend going over facts will be greatly reduced. With the content portion completed prior to the group meeting, your group time can emphasize the application of the biblical concepts to your individual members. A leader's guide is included at the back of the book to direct you in a review of the content. But the real strength of the leader's guide is to show you how to apply what you are learning. If you don't have the opportunity to go through this series with a group, that's OK too. Just be sure to think through all of the **Journey Inward** sections at the end of each session.

FROM THE AUTHORS

As you work through Book 3 in the **BibleLog** Series, expect to see a lot of contrasts. One you can't miss is God's love and perfection contrasted with mankind's sinfulness and disobedience.

Second, the Old Testament heroes and heroines, even with their many shortcomings, stand in bold contrast to the many wicked men you will read about. A third contrast to look for is in the results of choices. When a character chooses to do what God wants him or her to do, keep your eyes open for what happens to that character.

Contrast that person's life with a character who chooses not to do what God has instructed. Finally, look for comparisons and contrasts in your life and the lives of these Old Testament characters — both the good ones and the bad ones.

Here's a challenge to get you started, taken from the section of the Old Testament you are about to study.

> "Do not let this Book of the Law depart from your mouth; meditate on it day and night, so that you may be careful to do everything written in it. Then you will be prosperous and successful" (Joshua 1:8).

Pam & Stan Campbell

Destruction and devastation take place everyday.

1

THE FIFTH-CENTURY B.C. HOMECOMING PARADE

(Book of Ezra)

You see it regularly on the news. Destruction and devastation take place every day in a variety of ways and a multitude of locations. Floods and tornadoes wipe out entire towns. Plane crashes kill dozens, or even hundreds, at a time. Innocent children are shot as they play in their yards just because their house happens to be located near a war zone. Teenagers commit suicide and anguished parents keep asking themselves why.

Yet until you personally face a tragedy, it's hard to relate to the grieving people you see on your television. Since we are bombarded with *so much* bad news, it's almost impossible to empathize with all those people. That is, it's hard until *you* become involved in a similar situation. Only when you have been devastated in some way can you really relate to the feeling of having to start over from scratch (emotionally, financially, socially, or in any number of ways).

So before you get into this session, think of the worst tragedy you've ever had to face. How did you feel? How long did your feelings last? What did you do to overcome your feelings? How does that tragedy affect you even today?

By now you're probably thinking that this isn't the most fun way to begin a book—to recall the biggest tragedy in your life. But don't worry. The focus of this session will be positive, not negative. Sometimes you need to see how bad things can get before you can appreciate all the good things life has to offer. So keep your tragic experience in mind as you go through this session, and you'll be better able to relate to the content.

 **JOURNEY ONWARD**

If you went through Book 2 of this **BibleLog** series (*Who's Running This Kingdom?*), you no doubt remember the depressing story of how the kingdom of Israel had fallen. It had begun as a glorious, unbeatable nation led by God to victory after victory (under Kings Saul and David). It then became a showplace of wealth and wisdom (under King Solomon). But before long, Judah split from Israel. The individual kings started caring more about themselves than for God, whom they were supposed to represent. Idol worship became prominent. And even though God sent some of His boldest prophets (Elijah, Elisha, and others), the spiritual decay was too great. A few kings that followed Solomon were godly, but their positive influence was "too little too late."

Eventually God allowed Israel to be taken into captivity and exile by the Assyrians. And a few years later Judah was defeated by the Babylonians. The temple was burned and the walls of Jerusalem were torn down (2 Chronicles 36:19). King Zedekiah was blinded and carried off to Babylon in shackles (2 Kings 25:7). But we also noted that the Book of 2 Chronicles ends on a hopeful note that a Persian king named Cyrus would someday allow the rebuilding of the temple in Jerusalem (2 Chronicles 36:23). That's where the Book of Ezra begins.

Read Ezra 1:1-11.
About 70 years passed between the fall of Jerusalem and the beginning of the Book of Ezra. (The 70-year exile was predicted by the Prophet Jeremiah [Jeremiah 25:11-12], but we won't study his prophecy until Book 4, *Watchmen Who Wouldn't Quit*.) In that 70-year time period, the nation of Babylon was defeated by the Medes and Persians, which meant that the people of Judah (in exile) had new bosses. Review Ezra 1:1-4 and describe what kind of guy the new king (Cyrus) was.

The Fifth-Century B.C. Homecoming Parade

So with the blessing of the king, the exiles in Babylon began a homecoming parade back to Jerusalem (sometime between 559 B.C. and 530 B.C.). What was their mission? (Ezra 1:5)

What surprise gift did King Cyrus give them? (1:7)

Skim Ezra 2:1-70.
What groups of people and animals comprised Judah's homecoming parade? (2:64-67)

Read Ezra 3:1-13.
When everyone got to the Jerusalem area (after a 900-mile journey), they resettled in their original towns. They also started a collection for the rebuilding of the temple. Later they all gathered in Jerusalem to begin work on the temple. What was the first thing they rebuilt? (3:2-3)

Getting Personal — *Imagine being a part of Judah's homecoming. What would you have wanted to do as soon as you arrived home?*

You'll notice that the land was still inhabited by other peoples, and the returned people of Judah were a little scared of them. But that didn't keep them from getting to work and renewing their religious practices. One of the first things they celebrated was the Feast of Tabernacles (Ezra 3:4; Leviticus 23:33-43). How did they get the wood to restore the temple? (Ezra 3:7)

13

The work was supervised by Jeshua, the priest, and Zerubbabel, the leader of the people. After the foundations of the temple were laid, the people celebrated. But their emotions were mixed. Why? (3:10-13)

Here Comes Trouble
Read Ezra 4:1-24.
As the temple construction progressed, the people of Judah began to get attention from the surrounding peoples and began to encounter opposition. The first tactic of Judah's enemies was to try to infiltrate Judah's ranks. How did their plan work? (4:1-3)

What was the second attempt by Judah's enemies to oppose reconstruction of the temple? (4:4-5)

Getting Personal — *Do you ever sense opposition to your local church? If so, why do you think this occurs?*

Ezra 4:6-23 describes an incident from the reign of Artaxerxes, a king who followed Cyrus and Darius. The incident is inserted at this point to show us that the slander campaign against Judah continued for a long time. Apparently the enemies of Judah weren't very successful while Kings Cyrus and Darius were in charge. But they wrote a nasty letter to Artaxerxes accusing the people of Judah of several things. And the letter got his attention. What accusations were made against Judah? (4:11-16)

King Artaxerxes believed enough of what Judah's enemies said to issue a proclamation to halt the work being done to rebuild Jerusalem. (By the time

Artaxerxes was king, the temple had already been completed.) After he replied to the enemies of Judah, they went out and forced the people of Judah to stop what they were doing.

Read Ezra 5:1-17.
So first the opponents of Judah succeeded in temporarily halting work on the temple (4:24). And later, during the reign of Artaxerxes, they succeeded in postponing work on the city of Jerusalem. But what got the people of Judah started on the temple project again? (5:1-2)

According to the Book of Haggai, the outside interference wasn't the only thing that had slowed down the temple rebuilding project. The people of Judah were also preoccupied with their own homes. They finally started working again after God sent a drought, and after they were motivated by the preaching of Haggai and Zechariah.

When work on the temple began again, the local authorities (Tattenai and Shethar-Bozenai) wanted to know who had authorized Judah's return to work. They also wanted a list of names of the construction workers. But God was in control of the situation. Even though the local rulers gathered information, they didn't stop the people from working on the temple.

So the local authorities wrote to King Darius, asking for an official "Cease Building" proclamation. That letter is recorded in Ezra 5:7-17. Read it and answer the following questions:

❏ What reasons did the people of Judah give for rebuilding the temple?

❏ Did the people of Judah realize why God had allowed them to go into captivity? Explain.

❏ What did the local officials want King Darius to do?

Read Ezra 6:1-22.
Fortunately, it seems that the Persians kept pretty good records back then. A memo from King Cyrus was discovered that confirmed what the people of Judah had said (6:1-5). So King Darius wrote back to the local officials. What instructions did he give them? (6:6-10)

What would happen if King Darius' instructions were ignored? (6:11-12)

So with the approval of the Persian leaders and the motivation of the Prophets Haggai and Zechariah, the people zipped right through the rest of the temple construction. (The return to work began in the second year of the reign of King Darius [4:24], and the new temple was completed in the sixth year of the reign of Darius [6:15].) What activities took place at the dedication ceremony? (6:16-18)

After the temple was completed, the people began to live as they once had. They reinstituted the Passover celebration, the Feast of Unleavened Bread, and other of their ceremonies (6:19-22). And they weren't reluctant about it either. They were "filled with joy" because God had changed the attitude of the foreign kings and had brought His people home.

Getting Personal — *When was the last time you were "filled with joy"?*

Enter Ezra
Read Ezra 7:1-28.
It is at this point in the biblical narrative that Ezra himself comes into the

picture. While the temple reconstruction was going on, Ezra was still in Babylon. He got to Jerusalem about a year after the temple was completed. What kind of person was Ezra the priest? (7:6-10)

Ezra was accompanied by a variety of temple workers—priests, Levites, singers, gatekeepers, and servants. He also had a letter from King Artaxerxes. Basically, that letter served as a blank check to give Ezra whatever he needed to get the temple set up in Jerusalem (silver and gold, animals and materials for sacrifices, a "tax-free status" for the priests and temple workers, etc.). And the letter even gave Ezra authority beyond the realm of his own people. What did King Artaxerxes want Ezra to do? (7:25-26)

[NOTE: You may notice that Ezra refers to his people as "Israel" when actually "Judah" would be more technically correct. But it seems that Ezra's intention was to again unite the kingdom by including anyone from Israel *or* Judah who returned to Jerusalem from exile.]

Read Ezra 8:1-36.
The eighth chapter of Ezra is a more detailed flashback of Ezra's journey from Babylon to Jerusalem. Before his group left Babylon, they fasted and asked God for a safe trip. Then they wanted to show the king that they really trusted God to take care of them. How did they do that? (8:21-23)

Was their trust in God justified? (8:31-32)

17

Read Ezra 9:1-15.
But as soon as Ezra arrived in Jerusalem, he encountered a serious problem that would affect the spiritual condition of the recently returned people of God. What was the situation? (9:1-2)

What was Ezra's immediate reaction? (9:3-4)

Then what did Ezra do? (9:5-6)

Read Ezra 10:1-17.
Ezra's prayer was brutally honest (9:6-15). He made no attempt to justify the sinful actions and attitudes of his people. He didn't try to make the problem sound less severe than it really was. And even though *he* wasn't personally guilty of wrongdoing, his prayer was on behalf of *all* the people (including himself). What was one result of Ezra's prayer? (10:1)

After Ezra had demonstrated the magnitude of Judah's sin, a man named Shecaniah came up with a suggestion to solve the problem. What did he suggest? (10:2-4)

Shecaniah's proposed solution was a severe action for a severe problem. Yet Ezra saw wisdom in his proposal and acted on it while he continued to fast for Judah. A proclamation was then issued ordering everyone to assemble in

Jerusalem. What was the penalty for anyone who failed to comply? (10:7-8)

At the assembly, it was pouring rain. The rain depressed the people, and their reason for being there just made it worse. They realized that they were doing the right thing, but they also knew that the problem was too big to be taken care of in a day or two. So what did they decide to do? (10:9-17)

Skim Ezra 10:18-44.
If you count the names listed in Ezra 10:18-44, you'll find about 111 men who were guilty of marrying foreign, pagan wives. And even though some of these women had also borne children to the men of Judah, they were sent away. After all, intermarriage and idolatry were two practices largely responsible for the original downfall of Israel and Judah. There could be no tolerance for allowing the same thing to happen as soon as God led them out of exile. Their tragedy of Babylonian captivity was finally behind them, and they were determined to take any steps necessary to prevent the same thing from happening again.

The Book of Ezra seems to end rather abruptly at this point, but the same story is continued in Nehemiah, which you will cover in the next session.

 **JOURNEY INWARD**

The period of exile for the people of Judah taught them the importance of **starting over after failure.** This had to be one of the most traumatic periods in their history. Even in Egypt, they had started out in the good graces of the Egyptian government and had gradually been forced into slavery. In this case, however, they were in their own country—one they had fought to occupy and sweated to build. But when things got good and comfortable, they neglected the God who had made it all possible. As a result, they were invaded by foreign powers, yanked out of their homeland, and dragged away into captivity. They were in different surroundings, hearing different languages, and learning to cope with different (lower) social status. Only when they reached that bottom level could they realize that their God was great enough to lift them up from there and give them a brand-new start.

You can probably find some parallels between this story and the tragedy you listed at the beginning of this session. Some of the worst tragedies never make the national, state, or even local news. They are the personal tragedies we all face from time to time. So with your tragedy in mind, think through the following questions.

(1) When your life falls apart, how do you start over again?

(2) Why did your life fall apart to begin with? (List all the reasons you can think of.)

(3) After a crushing defeat, how do you keep your life from falling apart again?

As you answer these questions, keep in mind the following facts you should have learned from your tour through Ezra:

- ❑ God allows His people to experience occasional defeat, but those incidents should turn our attention back to Him. Defeat and tragedy are *temporary*.
- ❑ God willingly offers repentant people a fresh new start after their defeats.
- ❑ When you begin to start over, you can expect opposition from other people.
- ❑ It's easy to fall back into the same sinful habits that caused your defeat in the first place. So these are to be avoided at all costs.
- ❑ God is Lord over our major tragedies, not just "little" things like food, protection, and so forth. We should remove any mental limits we might be placing on His power.

Whatever crises you have been through, always keep in mind that God is aware of your situation and wants to help you start again. Your first step should be to follow Ezra's prayer example and let God know exactly how you feel. Don't dodge the blame for anything that might have been your fault. Only then will you be ready to let God give you the strength to start again. If you haven't yet taken that first step, there's no better time than right now.

 **KEY VERSE**

"The gracious hand of our God is on everyone who looks to Him, but His great anger is against all who forsake Him" (Ezra 8:22).

Nothing is quite good enough to please us.

2

WHEN THE WALLS CAME TUMBLIN' UP

(Book of Nehemiah)

All of us go through periods in our lives when our attitudes change. It's like we step through a doorway from innocence and childhood into . . . *The Criticism Zone*. All of a sudden, nothing is quite good enough to please us.

Often, this change of emphasis begins with ourselves. Mirrors become daily enemies as reflections portray noses we think are too large. Hair too unruly or not light enough. Stomachs that protrude too much. Chests that don't protrude enough. And so on and so on.

The usual reason we think such things is because we begin to notice people whom we think are a little better looking. Then we begin to compare ourselves to those people, and get depressed and self-critical. So unfortunately, for many of us the next step is to look for people who are worse off than we are and criticize *them*.

❏ "Have you ever seen such ratty-looking hair?"
❏ "If she's a real blond, I'm the Queen of the Universe."
❏ "Where does he shop for clothes? Salvation Army blue-light specials?"
❏ "She's too skinny."
❏ "He's such a big wimp."
❏ "They're so dumb."

Thankfully, this criticism kick is usually a phase most people quickly grow out of. But for some, it becomes a lifestyle. And then criticism really gets ugly. Children can *never* do the right things. All bosses become tyrants. Friends can never quite stack up to your expectations. And if a person's critical attitude is never dealt with, he or she is in for a life of frustration and unsatisfactory relationships.

So how can *you* avoid a lifetime of being trapped in *The Criticism Zone?* It's not easy, but *right now* you have to decide to stop being so critical. And then comes the really hard part: you have to learn to receive criticism without dishing it right back. But once you decide to do so, you will probably be surprised at how worthwhile and productive your life will become. At least, that was true for the main character in this session.

 **JOURNEY ONWARD**

Read Nehemiah 1:1-11.
As we said in the last session, the Book of Nehemiah picks up right where Ezra left off. The Book of Ezra began with the exiles in Babylon, who were leaving to rebuild the temple in Jerusalem. The Book of Nehemiah begins with Nehemiah in Babylon facing a slightly different problem. What was it? (Nehemiah 1:3)

How did Nehemiah respond when he heard about the problem? (1:4)

Getting Personal — *Put yourself in Nehemiah's place, and describe how you would have responded to his problem.*

What problems do you think an unwalled city might face during this time in history?

What was Nehemiah's job in Babylon, and what does it tell you about the kind of person he was? (1:11)

Read Nehemiah 2:1-16.
Nehemiah determined to ask permission to return to Jerusalem to do what he could to see that the wall around the city was restored. But before he could speak to the king, Artaxerxes was aware that something was wrong with Nehemiah. How could he tell? (2:1-2)

It took courage for Nehemiah to ask King Artaxerxes for such a large favor, but the king's initial response was favorable. A time was set for the trip, and then Nehemiah made some additional specific requests. What did he want from King Artaxerxes? (2:7-9)

Getting Personal – *What can we learn from Nehemiah about approaching those in authority over us?*

The king granted Nehemiah's requests, and things were looking pretty good. But meanwhile, back in the Promised Land, trouble was already a-stirrin'. What was the problem that was beginning to develop? (2:10)

Outside Opposition
Read Nehemiah 2:17-20.
When Nehemiah got to Jerusalem, he didn't announce his plans right away. He stayed for three days and then sneaked out one night to see how bad the problem really was. After getting a good feel for the size of the job ahead of him, he finally announced his plans to organize the reconstruction of the wall around Jerusalem. What was the response from the Jews? (2:17-18)

What was the response from the non-Jewish rulers of that area (Sanballat, Tobiah, and Geshem)? (2:19)

Read Nehemiah 3:1–4:23.
Nehemiah refused to give in to the jeers of his critics and expressed confidence that God would see him through the project. Then he divided his work force into separate crews and gave each crew a section of the wall to work on. (These work assignments are listed in Nehemiah 3.) But once the work got seriously underway, Nehemiah's opponents seriously increased their criticism. What was the mood of Sanballat and his cronies at this point? (4:1-3)

How did Nehemiah respond to this increased criticism? (4:4-5)

The work went well because "the people worked with all their heart" (4:6). Soon the bottom half of the wall was completed. But as the wall progressed, so did the criticism from Sanballat and the others who were opposing Nehemiah. What did the bad guys plan to do this time? (4:7-8)

And what did Nehemiah do? (4:9)

Getting Personal – *Do your coworkers or friends consider you a person who "works with all your heart"? Why or why not?*

Someone has said that when you try to serve God, you need to work as if it's all up to you and pray as if it's all up to God. That seemed to be Nehemiah's attitude. He prayed for help, but he also took a practical step to keep from being caught off guard. However, Nehemiah's problems were far from over.

When the Walls Came Tumblin' Up

The very next report he got listed three complaints from the people of Judah:

(1) We have too much rubble and too little strength to rebuild the wall (4:10).
(2) Our enemies say they're going to sneak in and kill us before we know what's going on (4:11).
(3) Our friends keep telling us it's no use—we're going to be attacked from all sides! (4:12)

That's all Nehemiah needed, right? His enemies were constantly criticizing him from outside and his own people were questioning him from within. You can probably imagine the rumors that would likely be spreading under such conditions. At this point, most of us would give up and go home. But not Nehemiah. He took several specific actions to rebuild the morale of his people. What things did he do? (4:13-23)

Inside Interference
Read Nehemiah 5:1-19.
Nehemiah's plans seemed to reduce the threat of outside interference, but he kept finding new problems among his own people. A famine had struck, and the economy was not good. To make things worse, the prosperous Jews were benefiting at the expense of the poorer ones. Several of the poorer people were mortgaging houses, fields, and vineyards just to buy food. Some were even forced to sell their children into slavery to non-Jewish people. And it seems that even the Jews who *were* loaning money to their neighbors were doing so in hopes of making a good profit on the interest. (Charging excessive interest rates on loans is known as *usury*, and was forbidden in the Old Testament law [Exodus 22:25-27].) What did Nehemiah ask of the people who were profiting from the suffering of others? (Nehemiah 5:6-11)

How did the wealthy people respond to Nehemiah's request? (5:12-13)

Getting Personal — *Why do you think it is so hard to be prosperous — and righteous? Do you consider yourself prosperous? Why or why not?*

Nehemiah went on to explain that as an official governor of the area, he was *entitled* to certain privileges. He *could* eat the finest foods and collect taxes from the people. But even though it would have been his *right* to do so, he chose not to. Why? (5:14-16)

Read Nehemiah 6:1-19.
The more Nehemiah struggled to keep his people working together to get the wall built, the harder Sanballat (and Nehemiah's other enemies) tried to stop their progress. What scheme did they use this time? (6:1-4)

The bad guys wouldn't quit trying. Sanballat finally sent a letter carried by his personal aide. The letter was an attempt to blackmail Nehemiah into meeting with Sanballat. The letter accused Nehemiah of planning to become king (which would have been greatly frowned upon by the *real* Persian king). How did Nehemiah respond to this threat? (6:8)

Nehemiah realized that all the criticisms and threats of his enemies were only attempts to get him so shaken up that he couldn't get any work done. How did he keep from giving in to his enemies' attacks? (6:9)

The next strategy of Sanballat was the most devious yet. What was his plan, and how well did it work? (6:10-13)

When the Walls Came Tumblin' Up

Believe it or not, the wall around Jerusalem was finally completed in spite of all the interference by Sanballat and his associates. With all the problems faced by Nehemiah, it seems that the job must have taken forever. But what was the actual amount of time it took to rebuild the wall? (6:15)

Did the completion of the wall actually matter that much to the surrounding nations? Why? (6:16)

Read Nehemiah 7:1-3.
After the wall was completed, Nehemiah appointed gatekeepers, singers, and priests. He put his brother, Hanani, and another man named Hananiah in charge of Jerusalem. How did he determine who would make a good leader? (7:1-2)

Getting Personal — *What do these verses indicate to you about the various roles of the people of God? Which of the three roles — gatekeeper, singer, priest — do you most identify with?*

Back to Basics
Skim Nehemiah 7:4-73.
Nehemiah 7:4-73 contains a list of the exiles who returned to Judah. (It's very similar to the list in Ezra 2.) They numbered 42,360 in addition to 7,337 servants and 245 singers.

Read Nehemiah 8:1-18.
After the wall was completed, the people all assembled in Jerusalem. Ezra was there to read the Book of the Law to the people. Review Nehemiah 8:1-6, then describe the scene and the people's reaction to Ezra's words.

The people wept as God's laws were read and explained. But Nehemiah, Ezra, and the Levites encouraged everyone to celebrate and be joyful. The people immediately began to put into practice the instructions that had been read to them from God's Word. What effect did their obedience have on them? (8:17-18)

Skim Nehemiah 9:1-38.
Later the people got together again to confess their sins (and those of the generations before them). They fasted, wore sackcloth, put dust on their heads, and worshiped God. Then the Levites led the people in a prayer that traced the entire history of the Israelites from creation to the present time (Nehemiah 9). After the prayer, the leaders of the nation all signed a written, binding agreement that they would continue to serve God.

Skim Nehemiah 10:1-39.
Review Nehemiah 10:30-39 and list some of the specific promises included in that agreement (especially note vv. 30-31, 35-37).

Skim Nehemiah 11:1-36.
A little later, another small problem came up. Apparently, the population of Jerusalem was not as large as it should be. There were plenty of people living in the area of Judah, but the city itself was understaffed. How was this problem resolved? (11:1-2)

Skim Nehemiah 12:1–13:31.
Nehemiah 12 contains some "odds and ends" information. The first 26 verses list the original priests and Levites who returned to Judah under the leadership of Zerubbabel. Verses 27-47 describe the dedication of the wall in Jerusalem. The description sounds like a modern-day parade with marching bands. Musical Levites were playing cymbals, harps, and lyres, while two large groups of singers (marching in different directions) walked the perimeter of the city on top of the wall. Then they met together and had a worship

service, complete with sacrifices. And that day they made a lot of noise (12:43).

Nehemiah 13 lists some of the official acts of Nehemiah after he had taken care of rebuilding the wall. One of the first things he did was a little housecleaning. He found out, much to his dismay, that one of the priests had supplied a room in the temple for Tobiah, one of Sanballat's allies who had caused the Jews so much trouble. The priest had emptied out provisions for the temple in order to give Nehemiah's enemy a place to live. What did Nehemiah do to resolve the problem? (13:8-9)

Nehemiah also made sure that the priests were provided for (13:10-13); prevented business from being transacted on the Sabbath (13:15-22); and chastised several of the men of Judah who had intermarried with pagan women (13:23-27). And after all Nehemiah had done, he was able to complete the account of his career with the words, "Remember me with favor, O my God" (13:30).

 **JOURNEY INWARD**

A close examination of Nehemiah's life can teach us a lot about **handling criticism.** He certainly had more than his fair share of critics who tried to keep him from accomplishing anything.

How about you? Think of the past three days (or maybe even just the past 24 hours), and try to recall all the criticism you have received. Don't forget to include criticism from your friends, children, spouse, boss, and anyone else you came into contact with. List their criticisms below.

Now review your list. Cross off any statements that are totally untrue. (You know, like, "You have the IQ of a small appliance bulb.") Put a dash (—) in front of the statements that are only partially true, or that you aren't sure of. (Partially true statement: "You try hard, but you'll never amount to anything." Unsure statement: "Son, I don't know what's going to become of you.") What's left will be the criticism you think is completely true.

If your list is like most, much of the criticism is totally untrue and most of the rest is shaky. If you're an accounting wizard or have a calculator handy, you might want to divide the number of true statements by the number of total statements to see what percentage of your criticism is worth listening to. But you probably won't need to discover the exact percentage to see that you should probably ignore much of the criticism you receive.

An even more important consideration is how you *feel* when people criticize you. How *do* you feel in those situations? Why do you think you feel that way? How long do your feelings last after being criticized?

Not all criticism is bad, of course. People who care will offer constructive criticism at times when they notice things that can improve our lives. And we should listen and take corrective action based on their observations. But too often it's the unjustified criticism that gets to us. That's when we need to remember Nehemiah.

How did Nehemiah handle criticism?

❑ *He knew truth from fiction.* He didn't believe every lie his enemies told him. Do you have enough confidence in yourself to know your own limitations, or do you let others decide what kind of person you should be?

❑ *He had definite goals.* He was determined to get that wall built, no matter what! Do you have specific goals in life, or are you always reacting to what other people think you should do?

When the Walls Came Tumblin' Up

❑ *He stuck to God's plan for him.* He knew that what he was doing was important to God. So when he was criticized, he just prayed and reminded himself that pleasing God was more important than pleasing people who didn't even like him. Are you more concerned with pleasing God or pleasing others?

You can build a wall in one of two ways. You can get with your Christian friends and family, work together, ignore criticism from others, and build a wall that will repel ungodly influences. Or you can listen to criticism and build a wall between yourself and everybody else. You're always going to have critics. Are you always going to have walls too?

 **KEY VERSE**
"Do not grieve, for the joy of the Lord is your strength" (Nehemiah 8:10).

Was the check just a lucky coincidence?

3

WHAT A COINCIDENCE!
(Book of Esther)

Imagine you or your spouse are in desperate need of a car. Let's say you could use some extra money, and if you had a car, you could commute to a good-paying job. So your spouse isn't opposed to buying a second car, but the money just isn't there to pay for one.

Then one day you hear of an incredible, one-time offer. (It's through a trusted friend, so you know you aren't going to get taken.) But if you can't raise $500 for a down payment by noon today, the opportunity is gone.

Your in-laws can't help you out. Your friends can't spare any money at the time either. Your cookie jar account comes to $137.19. As a last resort, you decide to pray for the money. (Yeah, you should have thought of this earlier, but you didn't.) So you ask God to somehow, some way, somewhere provide enough money for the car, and you give Him all the good reasons for needing it.

You try to help God out all you can, so you go through the pockets of all your seldom-worn clothes. You search under the cushions of your sofa and chairs. You look behind the refrigerator. But you can't find a single stray coin or bill anywhere.

You figure you'll go tell the car owner that it's no deal, and on the way you check the mailbox. A letter from a legal firm is there, addressed to you. As you shuffle off toward your destination, you rip open the envelope and wonder who is suing you. But then you stop still in your tracks! Enclosed is a check for $362.56 and a letter explaining that a distant uncle you never knew has died and included you in his will.

You put your vastly developed mental abilities to work and are just about to let God know He came up 25¢ short, when the sun reflects off a shiny object on the sidewalk. You pick up the quarter, stop for a few milliseconds to thank God, and then rush off to get the keys to your new car.

That afternoon as you drive your family or friends around town, you tell them of the remarkable miracle that God performed for you. But they don't agree with you. They point out that the letter was postmarked two days before you even prayed for the money. They say your receiving the money was coincidence. Fate. Luck. Would you agree with them? If not, what would you tell them to convince them otherwise?

It's not the purpose here to disprove the occurrence of random events. The laws of probability and statistics can be demonstrated with incredible accuracy. So sometimes things can happen "by coincidence." But it's also true that we miss out on too much of God's perfect timing because we're too quick to call it luck, good fortune, fate, or whatever.

If your spouse left a $50 bill on your dresser as a birthday present, and you tell him/her that, "By some lucky coincidence, a $50 bill appeared on my dresser," he/she misses out on the pleasure of giving, *and* you miss the joy of receiving. And a lot of times, God gives us wonderful surprises that we chalk up to fate. In today's session, we're going to see some "coincidences" that may cause us to think twice about concepts like luck, chance, and so forth.

 **JOURNEY ONWARD**
Read Esther 1:1-22.
The events of this session take place during the reign of King Xerxes, a Persian ruler who reigned after Cyrus and Darius, but before Artaxerxes. Xerxes seems to have been a flashy kind of guy. He ruled a large kingdom, and decided to have a huge exposition to display his kingdom's wealth and splendor. This display lasted 180 days and was capped off by a 7-day banquet. Xerxes' wife, Queen Vashti, had a separate banquet for the women.

What a Coincidence!

On the last day of the banquet, Xerxes decided he wanted to show off his wife in addition to the other fine things of the kingdom. (He had been drinking during this week-long banquet.) What happened when Xerxes sent for Vashti? (Esther 1:10-12)

[NOTE: A eunuch is a male who has had his sexual organs removed so that he can be trusted to attend to female royalty.]

Xerxes asked his advisers to consider what implications Queen Vashti's behavior might have, and what should be done with her. What did they advise? (1:15-20)

Read Esther 2:1-4.
Xerxes acted on his counselors' advice, but they weren't finished. What else did they suggest? (2:1-4)

Esther
Read Esther 2:5-23.
At this point, we meet the heroine of our story—a young girl named Esther. She had a male cousin named Mordecai who had raised her from a child (since her parents were dead). Esther and Mordecai were among the captives who were taken to Babylon when the Babylonians defeated Judah. Esther was also a good-looking young woman. Consequently, she was recruited when Xerxes' scouts went looking for young virgins who might be potential queens. What happened to her then? (2:8-14)

Getting Personal – *How do you think Esther felt when she moved from her family and community to Xerxes' palace?*

How did she do in her audition before King Xerxes? (2:15-18)

While Esther was inside the palace, Mordecai continued his life outside but kept up with her progress. Apparently no one connected the two of them, because no one realized that Esther was Jewish.

One day it just so happened that Mordecai overheard an assassination plot against King Xerxes. He passed the information on to Esther who passed it on to the king. The story was checked out and verified, the two conspirators were hanged, and the report was written up in the official records. It was sure a lucky coincidence that Mordecai overheard the plot, huh?

Read Esther 3:1-6.
Later, in a separate incident, Mordecai made an enemy. Who was the enemy, and how did the hostility get started between them? (3:1-5)

Mordecai's new enemy wasn't content just to confront Mordecai. What did he want to do? (3:6)

Holocaust B.C.
Read Esther 3:7-15.
Since Haman was close to King Xerxes, he approached him with a proposition. What did Haman suggest? (3:8-9)

What a Coincidence!

What was the king's answer? (3:11)

Read Esther 4:1-17.
Messages were sent to the leaders of Xerxes' provinces to have all the Jews put to death on a specific day in the near future. When Mordecai heard of the message, how did he respond? (4:1-3)

Esther heard that Mordecai was in mourning, but she didn't know why. (She hadn't heard of the king's orders to kill all the Jews.) So she sent a messenger to Mordecai to find out what was troubling him. Mordecai relayed all the exact details, and asked Esther to see if she could help from her position in the king's harem. Esther was a little reluctant to approach the king. Why? (4:9-11)

Getting Personal—*When faced with tough situations, how does your courage match up against that of Esther?*

Mordecai heard about her hesitation and sent another message to Esther. He pointed out that it was quite a "coincidence" that she had risen to such an influential position at this particular time. What was Esther's reply to this message? (4:15-16)

Read Esther 5:1-14.
In three days, Esther gathered her courage and went before King Xerxes.

What happened? (5:1-2)

Given the fact that the king was willing to grant any favor up to half of his kingdom, Esther's request was quite puny. What did she want from Xerxes? (5:3-8)

Haman was overjoyed when he heard about Esther's invitation. But his joy turned to rage as soon as he happened to see Mordecai. What advice did his wife and friends offer that made him happy? (5:9-14)

Tables Turn
Read Esther 6:1-14.
That night, by some "coincidence," King Xerxes couldn't sleep. By another "coincidence," he chose to read some of the official transcripts detailing the history of his kingdom. And he "happened" to read the account of how Mordecai had thwarted the assassination plot and saved the king's life.

When he discovered that nothing had been done to reward Mordecai, he determined to do something. By another incredible "coincidence," at that exact moment Haman walked into the palace to ask Xerxes if it would be OK to hang Mordecai on the new gallows Haman had just built. Before Haman could say anything, Xerxes asked, "What would you do if you were me and wanted to honor someone?" Well, proud Haman naturally thought the king was referring to *him*, so he laid it on thick. What did he advise the king to do? (6:6-9)

Then what happened? (6:10-14)

What a Coincidence!

Read Esther 7:1-10.
Haman had to rush right out from his humiliating experience to have dinner with Esther and the king. He was probably thinking about how much better he would feel after he got rid of Mordecai once and for all. But it wasn't one of his better dinners. As the three of them ate together, Xerxes again offered to grant anything Esther might ask—up to half of his kingdom. And at this strategic point, Esther told the king that someone had schemed to slaughter and wipe out her people. She said that even if her people had been made slaves, they wouldn't have complained to the king. But total annihilation was something they didn't deserve.

Xerxes asked Esther to identify the person who would dare do such a thing. The Bible doesn't say that she pointed a finger across the table, but she did identify the person as "this vile Haman" (7:6). At this point, what did King Xerxes do? (7:7)

What did Haman do? (7:7)

And as if the tension in the air weren't thick enough, Haman's "luck" went from bad to worse. What happened? (7:8)

And then one of the king's attendants spoke up and said something to the effect of, "What a coincidence. Haman just happens to have a gallows in his backyard." What happened then? (7:9-10)

Read Esther 8:1-6.
Esther inherited Haman's estate. Mordecai was brought before Xerxes and was given a signet ring. But still, all was not well. What else was Esther

concerned about? (8:1-3)

Purim
Read Esther 8:7-17.
Xerxes did more than grant Esther's request. Instead of writing an official decree himself, he left it up to Esther and Mordecai and agreed to sign and seal anything they wrote (8:8). What rights were the Jews to have under the decree written by Mordecai? (8:10-11)

How did Mordecai benefit from his experience with King Xerxes? (8:15)

How did the Jews respond to the amended decree? (8:16-17)

Read Esther 9:1–10:3.
What happened on the day that the enemies of the Jews had originally hoped to exterminate them? (9:1-5)

Haman's sons died on that day too, and their bodies were hanged on gallows as a public display (9:11-15). The victory of the Jews that day began an annual celebration called Purim (because Haman had cast a lot called a *pur* to determine on which day all the Jews would be executed—see Esther 3:7 and 9:24-27). And Mordecai became second in rank to King Xerxes himself.

So the Book of Esther has a happy ending. But had it not been for a few "random" events, the outcome might have been quite different. The question is: Were those random events just luck? Or was God involved at every step of the process?

What a Coincidence!

If you look for God's name in the Book of Esther, you won't find it. Yet this book as much as any other in the Bible shows how God works in the lives of His people. Mordecai was convinced that God would deliver the Jews in some way—perhaps through Esther, and if not, through someone else (4:14). And Mordecai was right. Because Esther had the courage to believe that God would protect her, she is remembered as a savior of her people. Her decision will never be forgotten.

JOURNEY INWARD

Now it's your turn. What have you decided about **coincidence, luck,** and **fate?** Our society is really geared to think in such terms. For example, in the two columns below, list all the things you can think of that are "lucky," or "unlucky." A couple are listed in each column to get you started.

Lucky Things	Unlucky Things
Four-leaf clovers Spilled salt over shoulder	Broken mirrors Walking under ladders

Now list all the events of the past week that you considered "lucky," "fortunate," or "coincidental." Consider gifts you may have received, relationships that are going your way, or close calls and near misses while driving, playing sports, etc.

The Book of James tells us that, "Every good and perfect gift is from above, coming down from the Father of the heavenly lights" (James 1:17). We need to become more aware that whenever something good happens to us, God was the source of the good event—not luck, fate, coincidence, or anything else. *Every* good gift is from God. For example, consider again the illustration that opened this session. Who's to say that God couldn't know in advance what you were going to ask Him two days later, and put in motion the answer to your prayer so that it would arrive just after you finally got around to asking? (You may have to think about that for a while.)

Every time you attribute something good to a source other than God, you rob yourself of the joy of receiving a gift from a loving Heavenly Father. Yet if you were to compare the amount of time you spend dwelling on your good (or bad) luck with the amount of time you spend in thanksgiving, you may discover that God isn't getting nearly the time He is due. So to end this session, think of the many good things you have in life. Then think of (and thank) the Source of those good gifts. You should experience a good feeling from giving credit where credit is due. And it won't be just a coincidence, either.

What a Coincidence!

KEY VERSE

"I will go to the king, even though it is against the law. And if I perish, I perish" (Esther 4:16).

Why do greedy people prosper while poor people starve?

4

WHAT DID I DO TO DESERVE THIS!?

(Job 1–31)

Sometime when you and a friend have 10 spare minutes, here are some questions for you to solve.

❏ Why do some really nice people die young, while some really rotten ones live long and apparently happy lives?
❏ Why do greedy people prosper while poor people starve?
❏ Why do some people go through intense pain before they die?
❏ Why are some people born with physical or mental handicaps?
❏ When plagues or disasters hit an area, why are some people spared when others die violent deaths?

These are tough questions because they question the nature of God. Underneath each of the previous questions is an unspoken assumption that a good, loving, fair God would not allow such things to happen if He could help it. And using that assumption, many people assume that either (1) God isn't good, loving, and fair, or (2) He is not powerful enough to prevent such things from happening.

The truth is that God is good, loving, fair, *and* powerful. He has promised to eventually set the record straight by using His power to set up a kingdom that is completely fair. But as long as we live in a sinful world, we must live with certain situations that are unfair. And sometimes, we are likely to wonder if God is really aware of what we're going through.

Such questions are not new. Neither is suffering. And whenever you combine your suffering with questions about the fairness and power of God, you find yourself in an old, old situation. This session will examine the old problem, yet in doing so you are likely to find answers for modern problems as well.

JOURNEY ONWARD

No doubt you've heard of Job. At least, you've probably heard of the patience of Job. You may even know about the problems he faced. But his struggle to find good advice may be a part of his life that you don't know too much about.

Read Job 1:1-22.
First, let's review his background. It is likely that Job lived prior to the kings and the judges—perhaps around the time of Abraham. He was from a place called Uz (not to be confused with Abraham's home, Ur).

What kind of lifestyle did Job have spiritually? (Job 1:1)

What kind of lifestyle did Job have materially? (1:2-3)

Job was also a family man. He had seven sons and three daughters and prayed for them regularly (1:2, 5). And God was pleased with Job. How can we tell? (1:6-8)

But because Job was such a good model of righteousness, he became a target for Satan. What did Satan propose to God? (1:9-11)

What condition did God place on Satan's proposal? (1:12)

What Did I Do to Deserve This!?

What happened to Job? (1:13-19)

What was Job's response? (1:20-22)

Read Job 2:1-10.
Even after Satan had taken away everything Job had, Job remained faithful. What second request did Satan make of God? (2:1-5)

What condition did God put on this second affliction? (2:6)

What happened to Job this time? (2:7-8)

What advice did Job get from his wife? (2:9)

Did Job take his wife's advice? Why? (2:10)

Getting Personal – *Who do you go to for advice in troubled times?*

Job's Comforters
Read Job 2:11-13.
Three of Job's friends heard about his troubles and decided to pay him a visit. Their names were Eliphaz, Bildad, and Zophar. How did they respond to Job's condition? (2:12)

What did they do to comfort Job? (2:13)

Getting Personal — *How do you try to comfort those going through hard times?*

Read Job 3:1-26.
Put yourself in Job's position. Suppose you're in the hospital and three of your friends come to see you. How would you feel if, when they saw how bad you looked, they started mourning and crying out loud? It probably wasn't exactly a pick-me-up for Job either. And then they sat there for an entire week without saying a word! (Their actions reveal a sensitivity to Job's situation, but Job would probably have liked some answers by then.) Job finally broke the silence. What did he say? (3:1-3, 11)

How was Job feeling at this point? (3:26)

Skim Job 4:1–6:30.
Eliphaz was the first of Job's friends to offer some advice. What did he advise Job to do? (4:1-7; 5:8, 17-18)

What did Job think about Eliphaz' advice? (6:14-17, 21, 24-25)

What was Job's attitude toward God? (6:8-10; 7:4-5, 16, 20-21)

Skim Job 8:1–11:20.
Bildad didn't appreciate the fact that Job was questioning God. What advice did he give Job? (8:1-6, 20-21)

Job agreed with Bildad, even though he didn't think Bildad provided the answers he was looking for. Job was beginning to feel frustrated and impatient with God. What were some of his accusations? (9:28–10:9)

Getting Personal – *Have you ever felt frustrated with God? What were the circumstances?*

Then it was Zophar's turn to speak, and he wasn't exactly sensitive to Job's problems. He assumed that Job was overlooking some specific sin and all he needed to do was tell God he was sorry. What were some of Zophar's comments? (11:4-6, 11, 20)

Skim Job 12:1–14:22.
Job replied that Zophar was telling him nothing new, but that he (Job) wasn't any worse a person than his three friends. He pointed out, among other things, that:

- He was a laughingstock to his friends (12:4).
- It's easy for people who don't have problems to criticize people who do (12:5).
- God knows what's going on even if people don't (12:13-25).

He also restated his desire to argue his case before God. How did Job further evaluate the advice of his friends? (13:4-5)

What additional requests did Job make of God? (13:20-24)

Round Two
Skim Job 15:1–18:21.
Eliphaz then spoke up again (Job 15). The first time he had been fairly kind to Job, but this time he sounded like he was running out of patience. He couldn't tolerate Job's questioning of God's judgment, and he just couldn't believe that Job would be suffering so if he hadn't done *something* wrong. How did Job respond to him, and what would Job do differently if Eliphaz were the one who was hurting? (16:1-5)

How did Job feel at this point? (16:15-17; 17:1-2)

Read Job 19:1-29.
Bildad spoke up and was angry at Job for being so hard on the three of them. Bildad was convinced that bad guys never prosper and good guys always come out OK. His speech is full of illustrations of things that will happen to evil people (Job 18). And Job couldn't seem to make him understand that he hadn't done anything worth the punishment he was receiving. (See 19:13-20 for a list of specific sufferings that Job was enduring.) What did Job want from his friends? (19:21-22)

And even though Job didn't understand why God saw fit to allow him to endure such a painful trial, what was his attitude toward God? (19:23-27)

Getting Personal – *What would your attitude have been?*

Job then issued a warning to his friends. What did he tell them? (19:28-29)

Skim Job 20:1–21:34.
Zophar reacted strongly to Job's warning. He gave another list of bad things that happen to wicked people, and seemed to suggest that since none of those things were happening to him that he must be more righteous than Job (20:1-29). Job again refuted his friend and insisted that he had seen plenty of instances where wicked people prospered. What were some of the specific examples he listed? (21:7-15)

Yet Job also realized that the prosperity of the wicked was not in their own hands, so he disregarded their advice (21:16). And after disagreeing with his friends, what did he tell them? (21:34)

Round Three
Skim Job 22:1–28:28.
Job's comments prompted Eliphaz to speak up for the third time. What he said this time was that God had no reason to notice someone who is doing the right thing. But when people begin to disobey, God will notice and reprimand them. Then Eliphaz accused Job (falsely) of some serious sins. What were they? (22:5-11)

And again, Eliphaz told Job that all he needed to do was admit his sins to God, accept God's instructions, and he would be delivered (22:22-30).

Job once more disagreed. He again said that if he could only state his case before God he would be justified. The problem was that he just couldn't seem to get God's attention—and it wasn't that he wasn't trying.

After all the suffering Job had gone through, had his feelings toward God changed much? (23:10-12)

At this point, Bildad took one more shot at offering advice to Job. He said it was silly for *any* person to claim to be pure in comparison to God (25:1-6). And Job's response was something to the effect of a sarcastic, "Duh. It sure takes a genius to figure that out" (26:1-4). (Job never claimed to be sinless. Yet he knew he had been in good standing with God and had no idea what he had done to deserve his recent suffering.) What else did he tell his friends? (27:5-6)

Job also realized that wisdom is a hard thing to discover. How *can* a person find wisdom? (28:12-28)

Skim Job 29:1–30:31.
As Job continued his speech (Job 29–30), he began to wish things were the way they used to be. He longed for the days when he was respected. When he and God had close fellowship. When he was able to help other people. And he contrasted those memories with his present situation when rude kids mocked and ridiculed him. When he was sick and terrified. When God seemed far away.

Finally, he went through a long list of possible sins and asked to be judged on each point.

Read Job 31:1-40.
Review Job 31 and list some of the specific wrongdoings that Job denied being involved in.

What Did I Do to Deserve This!?

With this final defense, Job ended his speech (and we end this session). In the next session you will discover that there was a fifth party sitting in on this conversation all along, and he wants a say in the matter. And of course, we kind of left Job sitting there in his suffering without any resolution to his problem. But now you'll have something to look forward to for next time.

JOURNEY INWARD

You might think that this first section of Job should end with a challenge to be more patient. But patience cannot be developed without some kind of crisis, so we first want to try to understand **suffering**. Back in Session 1, you named a tragedy that you have had to face during your life. Perhaps it came to mind again as you read through Job's saga. He had everything he could have wanted, and it seemed that he lost it all.

Job's sufferings were *physical* (painful sores), *emotional* (the deaths of his sons and daughters), and *spiritual* (God's apparent desertion in Job's time of need). What kinds of suffering do you sometimes endure in each of those categories? List your answers in the appropriate columns below.

PHYSICAL SUFFERING	EMOTIONAL SUFFERING	SPIRITUAL SUFFERING

Like Job's suffering, your suffering may raise some questions about the fairness of God. If so, try to maintain Job's attitude as well: "Shall we accept good from God, and not trouble?" (2:10) In the next session you'll see how God finally dealt with Job's questions. But first, write down any of your own questions that come to mind because of your suffering.

Finally, we shouldn't leave this session before seeing what we can learn about helping *other* people who go through periods of suffering. It's easy to get so caught up in our own problems that we ignore the pains of others. Certainly, Job's friends weren't the greatest help in the world, but they at least showed up when he was in misery. Do you notice when your friends or family are going through particularly trying times? And if you notice, can they count on you to be there and help see them through the hard times?

Notice that Job's three friends sat there for seven days without even saying a word. Sometimes that's all a friend can do. Even if you don't have any profound advice to offer, it's being there that's most important. Think of three people you know of right now that could use some encouragement. Write their names below, and before you begin the next session, do *something* to cheer them up (a card, a gift, a visit, etc.).

Who knows? When you begin to help other people through their times of suffering, your own sufferings may seem less severe. It's at least worth suffering through a try or two.

KEY VERSE
"Shall we accept good from God, and not trouble?" (Job 2:10)

What would you advise her to do?

5

STRAIGHT FROM THE SOURCE'S MOUTH

(Job 32–42)

Last week Jill had a small problem. She had decided to go back to college, so she was filling out some college applications and needed to list a couple of possible majors. But she hadn't yet decided for sure what field of education to pursue. She started to check the "Undecided" box, but she thought she would get some advice first. After all, she had just read in Proverbs that, "Plans fail for lack of counsel, but with many advisers they succeed" (15:22).

Now Jill has a *major* problem. The more people she talked to, the more different answers she got. Her best friend said, "You always did so well in English, and the stories you write are so good. Be a writer."

Her husband, a corporate vice president, advised her to go into business. He even promised to give her a good start in one of his company's offices. Her father, the Senator, thought the mayor's office could use a few good women. Her college-aged children said, "Go where the money is—doctor, lawyer, nuclear physicist, or pet cemetery owner." Her Sunday School teacher just knew Jill belonged on the mission field. And the more advice she received, the more confused Jill became.

The trouble was, no one really bothered to ask Jill what *she* wanted to do. If they had, she would have told them that she thought she wanted to teach elementary school kids (and had been thinking about it for almost a year). But now it seemed like such a small goal, after hearing what everyone else had in mind for her. She started to think it would be silly to go to college until she made up her mind. And she now had no idea when that might be.

59

If Jill were a friend of yours, what would *you* advise her to do? (Be sure to give her some good reasons to back up your suggestion.)

We all can get advice from a multitude of sources. The problem is that when those sources disagree, it's sometimes very hard to know which source to listen to.

JOURNEY ONWARD
Read Job 32:1-22.
In the last session you examined a dialogue (a rather *long* dialogue) between Job and his three friends on the topic of suffering. Job didn't have any answers to explain what had happened to him, and he didn't mind admitting it. But Eliphaz, Bildad, and Zophar weren't satisfied with saying, "We don't understand either." (They tried silence for a week, but then they started theorizing.) Their intentions were good, but they weren't much of a help to Job at all.

But there was another person sitting there, listening in on the whole conversation. His name was Elihu, and by now he was mad. Why was he angry at Job? (Job 32:1-2)

Why was he angry with Job's three friends? (32:3)

Why hadn't he spoken up sooner? (32:4-5)

What had Elihu come to realize about the source of wisdom and understanding? (32:6-9)

Elihu first addressed Eliphaz, Bildad, and Zophar. He pointed out that in all they had said, none of them had proven Job wrong or answered his arguments. He told them they couldn't claim to have found wisdom. But now that none of them had anything left to say, how did Elihu feel? (32:16-20)

Read Job 33:1-33.
Then Elihu spoke to Job. What was his attitude toward Job? (33:1-7)

Elihu first quotes Job's previous comments about being sinless and pure and Job's statement that God saw him as an enemy (33:8-11). Elihu explained that Job shouldn't complain about God's *actions* unless he fully understood God's *nature*. While Job complained that God wouldn't speak to him, Elihu pointed out that God might choose to speak in a number of ways. What are some of the ways that God might choose to communicate with people? (33:14-20)

Getting Personal – *How has God communicated to you?*

Elihu's Explanation
Elihu explained that there are reasons God may sometimes allow people to go through some rough times: (1) To turn them away from sin and its consequences (33:16-18); (2) to restore them to fellowship with God (33:26); (3) to remind people that no matter how good they are, they are sinful beings whom God never chastises to the extent that they deserve (33:27); and (4) to prove that He really loves them (33:29-30).

Read Job 34:1-37.
After talking to Job about God's actions, Elihu turned the discussion to God's nature. What did he tell Job about the nature of God? (34:10-15)

In his suffering, Job had been asking for a "trial" before God to argue his case. How did Elihu respond to that particular request? (34:21-30)

Skim Job 35:1–36:33.
Actually, Elihu was probably a little rougher on Job than Job deserved. He accused Job of "answering [God] like a wicked man" (34:36) and of adding rebellion to his sin (34:37). But Elihu was building a strong case for the justice of God. He went on to say that God is so far superior to man that man's actions, for good or bad, do not really alter God's basic nature (35:5-8). Yet God knows man's actions and responds accordingly. What is the eventual reward of people who remain righteous? (36:5-7)

And yes, said Elihu, God sometimes allows suffering. Why? (36:8-12)

When suffering comes, how do evil people respond? (36:13)

What effect should suffering have on godly people? (36:15-16)

Getting Personal – *How do you respond to suffering? How would others characterize your response?*

Skim Job 37:1-24.
Elihu reminds Job that God is the world's best teacher (36:22). We may not understand why He allows us to go through certain painful situations, but we can expect to learn valuable lessons from those situations. We can also count on God to see us through them. Elihu illustrated his concept of God's control of man by comparing it to God's control over nature—rain, lightning, thunder, wind, snow, and so forth (36:26–37:18). Finally, Elihu concludes his

speech to Job. What was his final point? (37:23-24)

God's Response
Read Job 38:1-38.
No record is given of Job's response to Elihu. Apparently, as soon as Elihu was finished speaking, God began to speak to Job. How did God appear to Job? (38:1)

God's eventual response to Job is interesting to note. He didn't come down hard on Job because of Job's confusion and honest questioning. But He didn't throw a pity party for Job either. God simply began to ask Job a series of questions. Job had previously sounded so authoritative about what God was like and what He should and shouldn't do. So when God spoke to Job, He gave Job an opportunity to show how smart he was in other areas as well. What did God ask Job first? (38:4-11)

After starting with "easy" questions like, "Where were you when I created the earth?" and "How would you like to try to keep the ocean from covering the land masses?" God asked Job to contemplate some harder ones. For instance: "Job, how would you like to create a morning, complete with sunrise at dawn?" (38:12-13) "Have you been down lately to see the underwater sources of the seas?" (38:16) "What do you know about what lies beyond death?" (38:17) "Where do you think I store light, darkness, snow, hail, and lightning?" (38:19-30) "What can you do to alter the constellations I've created?" (38:31-33)

Read Job 38:1–39:30.
After God focused Job's attention on the daily miracles of nature, He then directed Job's thoughts to the animal world. Job had probably been concentrating so much on himself that he neglected to consider the numerous other creatures in the world. So God continued His questioning to help make Job aware that He was concerned with *all* of His creation. (And since God takes care of all these wild animals, how much more will He watch over human beings?) What were some of the specific examples that God used

from the animal world? (38:39–39:30)

Getting Personal – *What are some daily miracles of nature that you are aware of? How does God take care of His creation?*

Read Job 40:1-24.
After this long flurry of questions (38:1–39:30), God paused and challenged Job to answer Him. How did Job respond? (40:1-5)

When God continued, He went right back to the question approach. What did God accuse Job of doing? (40:6-8)

Then God pointed out two more specific animals for Job to consider. The first is referred to as the "behemoth" (40:15). (The definition of *behemoth* in the original language is something like "mighty beast.") Opinions vary as to what specific animal this Bible passage refers to. The most common guess is that the "behemoth" is the hippopotamus. Other Bible scholars have proposed that it could be an elephant, rhinoceros, water buffalo, or even a brontosaurus. Review the description of this animal in Job 40:15-24 and describe it below.

The other animal God pointed out to Job also has a peculiar name—*leviathan*. This animal is also referred to in Psalms (74:14; 104:26) and Isaiah (27:1). It is apparently a sea animal, and some have supposed it to be a dolphin, whale, or marine dinosaur. However, the most widely accepted belief is that the leviathan was actually a crocodile. And since Job lived in the days before anyone was "smart" enough to invent alligator wrestling, crocodiles were creatures to be avoided.

Skim Job 41:1-34.
God first asked Job if he wanted to go try to capture a leviathan by force (41:1-4). Obviously, the answer was no. Then God asked Job if he wanted to go be nice to a leviathan and try to convince it to be a pet (41:5). Again, the likelihood of doing so was slim. What did God say would happen if Job tried one of these approaches? (41:8)

Then God raises an interesting question to the effect of: "If you aren't able or willing to stand against one of My creatures, what makes you think you're able to stand against Me?" God continued His description of the leviathan (41:12-34) and then gave Job another opportunity to respond to what had been said.

Job's Reply
Read Job 42:1-17.
What had Job come to realize about God? (42:1-2)

What confession did Job make to God? (42:3-4)

Job said that previously he had only heard of God. But after his suffering and his intense questioning by God, how had his attitude toward God changed? (42:5-6)

Remember that Job hadn't been a spiritual slouch *before* his suffering ordeal. He was faithful, prosperous, and a good example to everyone around him. God was even able to point to Job as an example of a devout man. But even though he was close to God when everything was going well, he became even better aware of who God really was through his painful suffering.

The Book of Job could have ended right here, leaving Job with an increased awareness of the majesty of God. But it doesn't. After Job saw the vast difference between himself and God (and repented), God spoke to someone else. Who? (42:7)

What were God's instructions? Why? (42:7-9)

But the story is still not over. The Book of Job has an all-lived-happily-ever-after ending. Review Job 42:10-15 and list the things that happened to Job during the later years of his life (after the suffering).

God also gave Job time to enjoy the blessings of his later life. Job lived 140 years after his period of suffering. And the last we hear of him is that, "he died old and full of years" (42:17).

JOURNEY INWARD

You may have noticed that Job asked a lot of questions that God never answered. But after Job saw more of God as He really is, his questions (and his suffering) didn't seem as significant as they had before. It was enough for Job to choose to remain faithful to God—no matter what. But if Job hadn't waited for God and had acted on some of the advice he had received earlier, his story could have had quite a different ending. So spend a few minutes before closing this session thinking about **where you get advice.**

First, make a list of all your sources of advice. You should come up with at least a dozen. (They don't all have to be people.)

SOURCE #1—

SOURCE #2—

SOURCE #3—

SOURCE #4—

SOURCE #5—

SOURCE #6—

SOURCE #7—

SOURCE #8—

SOURCE #9—

SOURCE #10—

SOURCE #11—

SOURCE #12—

Now go back and evaluate each source you listed. Write a percentage beside each source to indicate how reliable that source is. (50% = Reliable advice half the time; 100% = Reliable advice all the time.) By doing so, you will see which sources you feel are most trustworthy.

But it is then essential to check and see if you put a priority on the sources that are indeed most reliable. For example, it's hoped that you listed the Bible as a source of advice that is 100% reliable. And maybe you listed "friends" at 75% reliability. Consequently, when you need advice, you would do well to start with the Bible (even though you may be able to get good advice from friends as well). But in reality, many times we start with our other (less reliable) sources and hope the Bible agrees.

If you go back to this session's opening example about Jill's search for good advice, you'll notice that she consulted a lot of sources—friends, spouse, and children. And true, the Bible says to get a lot of input if you want the best possible plans. But be honest with yourself. Do you always search for the *best* advice? Or do you sometimes try to find sources of advice that support what *you* want to do?

Just getting a lot of advice is no insurance that the advice will be good. So if you are tempted to take an easy way out to avoid getting the best advice available, take a lesson from Job:

- ❏ *Don't be controlled by your feelings.* Job was crushed because of all the terrible things that happened to him, but he didn't give in to his emotions.
- ❏ *The first advice you receive may not be the best.* If Job had listened to his wife (2:9), his book of the Bible would be a lot shorter.
- ❏ *Majority doesn't always rule.* Job's three friends had a lot to say, but they didn't really have a grasp of his situation. Elihu was a minority, but his advice was much better than that of the other three.
- ❏ *Young people can be good advisers.* Age often brings experience and wisdom. But evaluate all the advice you receive, and don't disregard any just because of the age or position of the giver.
- ❏ *Don't limit yourself to human advice.* Job wasn't satisfied with the advice of his three friends, and he hung in there until God finally spoke and set him straight. Likewise, we always do better to consider God's advice before we act on any problem.
- ❏ *When you just can't find answers for your questions, remain faithful.* Face it,

there are certain questions that will probably go unanswered throughout your lifetime. Job never got all the answers he was looking for, but he received more than enough from God to go ahead with his life. The fact that you don't understand God's actions doesn't mean He's doing something wrong.

If you still have hard questions that you wish God would answer, keep searching. In fact, the focus of Session 7 is going to be honesty with God. God never faulted Job for his questions, just for a slightly improper attitude while he was asking them. If you're honest with God and make Him your #1 source of advice, you may be surprised how much you can "suffer" through without giving up. But you'll never know till you try.

KEY VERSE

"The Almighty is beyond our reach and exalted in power; in His justice and great righteousness, He does not oppress" (Job 37:23).

God is like . . . .

6

INTRO TO OLD TESTAMENT LIT.
(Assorted passages from the Psalms)

If you are like most people, at some point in your life you and your friends sat around late one night and carried on a long discussion about what God is like. And as you talked, you probably came up with some pretty standard images:

- ❏ A grandfatherly person who lives in heaven and would never harm anyone.
- ❏ A judge who will someday let us know everything we did right or wrong during our lifetimes—and who then will pass sentence on us.
- ❏ A gift-giver who works something like a vending machine. All we do is ask, and He gladly drops material goods from the sky into our laps.
- ❏ A Zeus-type figure who sits on the nearest mountaintop with an assortment of thunderbolts, waiting to zap us whenever we make a wrong move.
- ❏ Other (Add your own description):

The problem with trying to imagine exactly what God is like, is that God is much more complex than we can imagine. And while we sometimes debate back and forth whether God is loving and giving or whether He is vengeful and judgmental, the truth is, He is both. When talking about people, we assume that an individual has to be one way or the other. We usually can't comprehend a Being who can practice both perfect love and perfect justice. But the nature of God is so complex that our best efforts to understand it always fall short. (Remember Job's experience while trying to figure God out?)

By the end of this session, you will have a better image of what God is like — not because you will have found a *single* characteristic that makes Him who He is, but rather because you will discover *many* images that combine to form a character unlike any other.

JOURNEY ONWARD

In this session, we begin a study of the Psalms that will be continued in Sessions 7 and 8. Don't panic if you are aware that there are 150 psalms in all. We're not going to try to cover 50 per session. But you *will* have the opportunity to cover enough psalms to see why they have survived the years and are, for many people, among the best-loved passages of Scripture.

The Psalms are a diverse collection of writings by different people. Many were written by David; other writers included Asaph (one of David's choir leaders), Solomon, and Moses. Some psalms were written as songs. Some are prayers. Others are notes of praise and thanksgiving. Some were meant to be used in large groups. Some are private confessions by an individual. But the common theme that comes through loud and clear is that the Psalms are appeals to God.

Because the psalm writers used a lot of poetic language and imagery, some people love to read through the Psalms while others find it hard to appreciate them. But whether or not you usually appreciate similes, metaphors, and other poetic contraptions, you will learn much from the content of the different psalms. For one thing, since the writers took poetic license, they were able to describe God in ways that you may not ever have considered. This session will give you the opportunity to see a number of images of God as you study the descriptions provided by the psalm writers.

Power and Majesty

As you might expect, many of the descriptions of God refer to His power and majesty, so we'll start there. Read through each of the following references and record how the writer portrayed God. You may find a *description* of God, and you can include that. But more importantly, try to identify the *symbol* or *personification* of God as recorded by the author. (Most of these roles are plainly stated and easy to record. But in a few cases, the description is inferred, and you'll need to look a little harder and come up with your own interpretation of the passage. As an example, the first one has been completed for you.)

❏ Psalms 8:1-4; 95:6—These verses refer to God's forming of the universe and making mankind, so God is portrayed as a **Creator**.

❏ 7:6-9

❏ 10:16-18

❏ 18:28-29, 32

❏ 27:1

❏ 49:12-15

❏ 58:10; 94:1-2

73

Getting Personal – *Do you usually think of God as majestic and powerful? Why or why not?*

Military Images

If you worked your way through Book 2, *Who's Running This Kingdom?* you'll remember many of the exploits of David. Even before David became king, he proved himself to be a good soldier and mighty warrior. As a young boy he stood firm against Goliath. Later he remained faithful to God and successfully avoided the pursuits of King Saul, who wanted him dead. And even as king, David was an effective military leader.

Consequently, when David sat down to write a psalm, it was natural for him to refer to God by using a lot of military images. Many of David's psalms recall specific, personal instances when God's deliverance had saved his life. In other places, David speaks for the nation as he writes of God's protection. You should find samples of both personal and national examples as you research the following "military" images of God.

❏ Psalms 3:1-4; 7:10

❏ 7:12-13; 35:1-3

❏ 68:4-6

❏ 91:11-12

❏ 91:14

❏ 93:1-2

❏ 94:16-19

Getting Personal – *Do you usually think of God as a military leader? Why or why not?*

As you have seen, the Psalms contain many military and authoritative images of God, but they also abound in other images. Sure, God can (and should) be perceived as glorious and powerful. Yes, He can also be portrayed as a military figure to be obeyed and followed—no questions asked. But if we thought of God *only* in such terms, we would limit His nature and miss out on much that He has to offer us.

Relationships
The psalm writers know that God played many roles other than king, creator, redeemer, warrior, and the like. They realized that He originates other, more personal roles in His relationships with people. Read the following verses and record some of the personal, compassionate relationships God chooses to have with us.

- Psalm 18:16-17

- 20:4-5

- 23:1-2

- 25:8

- 25:9

- 34:4-7, 15-18

- 42:1-2

❏ 65:9-13

❏ 91:3-4

Getting Personal — *How would you describe your relationship with God?*

Assurance

Still another way the writers of the Psalms came to think about God was to look around them and observe objects of value or assurance, and then compare God's attributes to those objects. For example, the author of Psalm 66 must have seen a silversmith at work, melting down the ore until all the impurities were out of it and only the pure silver remained. Then, when thinking about God, the author was inspired to write: "You, O God, tested us; You refined us like silver. . . .We went through fire and water, but You brought us to a place of abundance" (vv. 10, 12). In other words, after observing what it took to get shiny silver from raw ore, the psalm writer could see that God the Refiner sometimes allows His people to "take a little heat" so they will reach their true value.

Read through the following verses, and list the people or objects to which God is compared.

❏ Psalm 9:9

❏ 18:46

❏ 24:1

❏ 40:3

❏ 56:8

- ❑ 63:1, 4-5

- ❑ 84:11

- ❑ 91:9-10

As you can tell, the psalm writers had a vast variety of images of God. They weren't content with assuming that God was a big, undefined presence "out there somewhere." Instead, as they went about living their lives, they looked for ways to expand their understanding of God. So after a while, God became to them like a rock, a fortress, a feast, a sun, a mother bird, and so forth. They began to realize that any source of comfort, security, or joy could be traced back to the God who loved them.

This session has barely scratched the surface of the Psalms, but it's an important beginning to understanding what the Psalms are really about. The next two sessions will give you opportunity to go a little deeper into the individual psalms. But before you do, you may need to widen your thinking when it comes to considering God's nature.

And by the way, this session begins a section of the Bible that consists of literature written during the times of the kings of Israel and Judah. (Many of the psalms are attributed to David; much of the content of Proverbs, Ecclesiastes, and Song of Songs is credited to Solomon.) Consequently, these next few sessions won't have a running plot and regular cast of characters like most of the previous sessions have. So don't ask yourself, *What events are taking place now, and what people should I remember?* Instead, ask, *What did these authors write down that I should remember and apply to my life?*

JOURNEY INWARD

Were you surprised at the number of **images of God** you found recorded in the Psalms? Why or why not?

Did any of them seem strange to you, or make you feel uncomfortable? Explain.

Which three of the images of God listed in this session are closest to your own concept of God?

To close this session, come up with at least three additional images of God, and explain the significance of each one. These should be examples that apply specifically to you. For example, someone who has been recently cured after a long illness might compare God to a doctor, a healer, or strong medicine that cures not only sickness but sin as well. An athlete might speak in terms of God being a coach—pulling His team (the church) together and leading it to victory. Record *your* three examples (and explanations) below.

Can you think of any time this past week when you would have found it comforting to think about God in one of the personal ways you just listed? Or as a Father, a fortress, a shepherd, or so forth? Be specific.

Finally, spend some time this week just meditating on the complex nature of God. If He seems impersonal and distant, it's not *His* fault. Perhaps *you* need to learn to think of Him on a much larger scale than you've been doing so far. Give it a try, and you'll soon discover that He can be everything to you that you could ever need or want.

KEY VERSE

"The Lord is my light and my salvation—whom shall I fear? The Lord is the stronghold of my life—of whom shall I be afraid?" (Psalm 27:1)

"I blasted it with my GI Joe cap pistol."

7

HONEST TO GOD

(Assorted passages
from the Book of Psalms)

A pastor paid a visit to a woman whose young son was playing in the backyard. After a while the boy rushed in, slinging a dead mouse by its tail. Not seeing the pastor, the child ran to his mother and said, "Look, Mommy. I just killed a mousie. First I crunched it with my baseball bat. Then I mutilated it with my bicycle. Then I blasted it with my GI Joe cap pistol. And then. . . ." At that point the boy saw the pastor, softened his voice, and said without hesitation, "And then he went to be with the Lord."

You've probably noticed how some people use a completely different language around their friends than they do around parents, church leaders, or other authority figures. And it's not just little kids. Take the Eddie Haskell character on "Leave It to Beaver," for instance. Eddie was a totally rotten high schooler, but anytime he was around Mr. or Mrs. Cleaver, he wore a big smile and turned on the flattery.

Even *you* may be guilty of misrepresenting yourself. Would any of the slang phrases and informal language you use with your friends make you uncomfortable if they were overheard by your pastor? Do you even discuss the same topics of conversation with your church friends that you do with coworkers? When some of us are with our peers, we talk about good-looking members of the opposite sex, our hopes and dreams for the future, God, death, and other major subjects of interest. But as soon as we get around certain other people, we seem to get speech amnesia—we apparently lose all ability to communicate verbally.

On the other hand, others of us are skilled at fooling authority figures. (All you Eddie Haskells raise your hands.) We crank up the charm when we know certain folks are looking and listening. And we say only what we know those folks want to hear. The problem with this attitude is that we often carry it over into our relationships with God. Since we aren't ever completely honest with others, it's really hard to open up and tell God exactly what we are thinking and feeling.

Added to that problem is the fact that most of us are taught *exactly* what to pray, and these "practice" prayers hardly ever include room for doubts or questions. So as people get older, they generally experience two problems related to prayer: (1) They don't do enough of it, and (2) Too much of what they do lacks genuine sincerity. Most people's prayers could include a little less automatic pilot and a little more honest conversation.

JOURNEY ONWARD

If the Psalms are any indication, God apparently doesn't mind honest expression. It should be noted up front, however, that being honest with God doesn't mean we have the right to be abusive or disrespectful. Even though the psalm writers were pretty bold with some of the things they said, their words were always backed up with praise and worship. They questioned God, complained to God, griped, whined, and made accusations to God. But it is clear from their writings that in spite of their words and feelings, they knew clearly that God was in control of their (and every other) situation. So as we go through this session, don't look for a license to attack God with unfounded charges. Your goal should be honest communication, not sarcasm or a defense of your improper behavior.

Many of the psalms were written when the writers were depressed or threatened. And they didn't beat around the bush like we might do. ("Dear God, I love You and praise You. I thank You for all the wonderful things in my life. And, oh yeah, by the way, I hate my job, and my wife and I are fighting a lot, and I think I have an ulcer, and my life is a complete mess. But I know You're busy, so don't worry about me. I'll be OK—that is, if I live through all this. Amen.")

Bold Requests

Read the following verses from Psalms and record the writer's request of God and/or his emotional state. (In some cases, you may not find both.)

	REQUEST	EMOTIONAL STATE
3:1-2, 5-7		
4:1		
9:13-14		
11:1-3		
25:7		
25:16-21		
31:9-14		

	REQUEST	**EMOTIONAL STATE**
40:11-12		
43:1-5		
54:3-4		
80:3-6		

Getting Personal – *How would you describe your current emotional state?*

Bold Complaints

As you can see, the psalm writers didn't mind telling God about all the painful experiences they were facing. And apparently they weren't much different than we are—whenever they were suffering, they didn't like to wait long for God to act. They wanted relief right away. Read the following verses from Psalms and write down the author's complaint in each case.

❏ 6:1-10

❏ 10:1

Honest to God

- ❏ 13:1-4

- ❏ 35:11-25

- ❏ 38:1-22

- ❏ 42:9-10

- ❏ 44:9-26 (esp. v. 23)

- ❏ 69:1-4

- ❏ 69:6-12

- ❏ 73:1-14

- ❑ 77:7-9

- ❑ 79:1-5

- ❑ 82:2

- ❑ 109:1-5

- ❑ 143:3-6

Getting Personal – *What current complaints do you need to bring to God?*

No doubt you've noticed that many of the requests had to do with persecution and God's seeming lack of concern for His people. Again, the writers knew God was there and that He had the power to act. They weren't challenging God's ability to straighten out unfair situations, but they *did* wonder why God allowed such unjust matters to continue for so long. Yet at the same time, they knew how things were going to work out in the long run. David expressed it well in Psalm 37:1-4. What would be the ultimate difference between evil people and godly people?

Honest to God

David had good reason to be so bold in his prayers to God. Read Psalm 26 and explain why you think David was able to be completely honest with God.

As you can see, openness in prayer depends heavily on living a righteous lifestyle. But what happens if you haven't been doing that? What if you are aware of sin in your life?

Bold Confession

Well, if *you* are aware of sin in your life, you can be sure that *God* is aware of sin in your life. And again, honesty in prayer is essential. One of the most famous sins in the Bible (if sins can be "famous") was David's adultery with Bathsheba and his murder of her husband, Uriah, to cover it up (2 Samuel 11). David became involved with sin in a major way. But just as he sinned intensely, he also repented intensely. Psalm 51 was written after David had been confronted with his sin by the Prophet Nathan.

What did David ask of God? (51:1-2)

Did David try at all to cover his sin or make it sound less severe than it actually was? (51:3-4)

Did David really expect God to forgive such a major blunder? (51:10-12)

Could any good possibly come out of David's sin? (51:13)

What did David realize that God wanted from him after his sin? (51:16-17)

Getting Personal – *Do you need to make any "bold confessions" to God?*

You've seen that it is OK to approach God with honest statements and requests—even if some of them seem severe. But the other side of honesty before God is shown in Psalm 51. Bold declarations and requests are all right, but they must be preceded by bold confession if we expect God to hear and respond to us.

Putting It All Together

Yes, it's important to be totally honest with God when you talk to Him. Yes, it's essential that you be just as honest about your shortcomings as you are about your requests. But one question remains: *When* do you express all this honesty? People have all sorts of strange habits when it comes to talking with God. Some people assume God is so busy that they shouldn't "bother" Him except in the event of extreme emergencies. Others ignore God during the good times, and then feel too guilty to ask for help during crises. (That's when all that honest confession comes in handy.)

Most of us need to practice getting to the point where we have a regular relationship with God. And our goal in prayer should be to feel as comfortable communicating with God as we do talking to our best friends. That means prayer should be:

- *Frequent*—How do you expect to have a good relationship without regular communication?
- *Eagerly anticipated*—If you dread prayer, it will never become a habit.
- *Not dependent on your mood*—Even when you don't feel like it, pray. Like a talk with a good friend, prayer should reflect whatever you are feeling: joy, despair, fear, or whatever.
- *Transforming*—Prayer should make a difference in your life. (You may not sense much of a change immediately, or even after a prayer or two. But the regular practice of prayer will eventually make a dynamic impact on your life.)

Honest to God

Does prayer *really* make a difference? As only one example of many, many others to be found in Psalms, take a look at Psalm 102. In what state of mind was the writer when he began his prayer? (102:1-2)

What were some of his specific concerns? (102:3-11)

During his cry to God, what did the writer begin to think about? (102:12-13)

In what state of mind was the writer when he ended his prayer? (102:25-28)

It's hard to conceive of anyone being much worse off than this psalm writer. His opening focus was on himself and his many problems. But the mere exercise of honestly expressing himself to God was enough to shift his thoughts from his own problems and shortcomings to God's ability to handle those very problems. In fact, halfway through the prayer the writer was already concerned that people who weren't even born yet would find reason to praise God (102:18). So even though this writer probably didn't *feel* like praying, the fact that he did so anyway really changed his outlook on life.

JOURNEY INWARD

How long has it been since you evaluated your **prayer habits**? If it has been a while, think through the following questions.

- ❏ If you took the exact amount of time and effort that you put into prayer, and spent *only that much* time and effort in your relationship with your best friend or spouse, how strong do you think that relationship would be after a month?

❏ What specific benefits have you received from prayer during the past month? (If you can't list a dozen or so, you probably need to work at it a little harder.)

❏ Evaluate your praying by placing an "X" at the appropriate place on each of the following lines:

My prayers are:

Meaningful_____Just a ritual

My prayers to God are:

Open and honest   What I think God
communication_____wants to hear

When it comes to confession, I try to:

Be completely   Forget about a
honest_____lot of my sin

When I'm really depressed, I:

Find it easy   Find it very hard
to pray_____to pray

Honest to God

Sometimes the hardest part about developing an open and honest relationship with God is getting started. Like any other relationship, you have to invest time in it and commit to keep it going. Perhaps you already spend a half-hour or so *every day* in prayer. If not, that's the first step you need to take. But then remember that just praying isn't enough. As you pray this week, strive for *total* honesty.

The phrase used as this chapter title, "Honest to God," is often used inappropriately as an oath. But from now on when you hear the phrase, think of it as a challenge. You can and should be "honest to God." In fact, it's the only way to insure a healthy spiritual life and a maturing outlook on who God really is. You won't be sorry. Honest.

KEY VERSE

"Search me, O God, and know my heart; test me and know my anxious thoughts. See if there is any offensive way in me, and lead me in the way everlasting" (Psalm 139:23-24).

No matter where you go, music starts to play.

8
JERUSALEM BANDSTAND
(Psalms 1, 8, 23, 24, 27, 63, 100, 119, 121, 139)

Imagine for a moment that you are a psychiatrist. One day a young woman dashes into your office and says, "Oh doctor, doctor, you've got to help me. Everywhere I go I hear voices and noises in my head. No matter what I do, I can't get rid of them. I wouldn't mind so much if they always said the same thing, but they don't. Most of the time the voices are harmless. Many times they're even helpful. They cheer me up and keep me from feeling lonely. They help me think big thoughts and imagine grand things. But just when I start to feel like I can't live without my little voices, all of a sudden they suggest that I do something bad. They begin to give me conflicting advice—some tell me to do good and others tell me that being good is a waste of time. Doctor, you're a professional. I need help. What should I do?"

Well, you're the doctor. What advice would you give this lady?

Have you ever known anyone with the symptoms this lady is experiencing? If not, you must live in a cave on some deserted island. Consider the impact of *music* on your life. Doesn't it fit the young woman's description? Most families have two or more radios on which they can tune in to any number of stations—24 hours a day. You get in the car. CLICK. Instant music. There are waterproof radios for when you're in the shower or the pool. There are tiny radios you can wear when you're jogging or exercising. You step in an elevator; music starts to play. You call your doctor and get put on hold, and music pipes in to help you pass the time. In malls, offices, and restaurants, music beams, blares, and beckons.

And if you don't like the music the disc jockeys are playing, forget the radios. Just grab a Walkman, borrow a tape deck, or buy a CD player. Then you can listen to what *you* want to hear. But even though you try to regulate the music you listen to, from time to time you're bound to hear "voices" that contradict what you've been taught is right and proper. Then what do you do?

JOURNEY ONWARD

Music has always been a major influence in society. Even in the fourth chapter of Genesis, mention is made of a man named Jubal, "the father of all who play the harp and flute" (4:21). Music was part of many of the Old Testament worship services. And the very fact that the Bible contains the Book of Psalms shows how significant music can be.

So with that in mind, let's go way back to some of the earliest hits that have survived the turntables of time. None of the other songs you've heard lately have lasted nearly as long. The list of 10 top psalms will vary from person to person, but the ones that follow are on a lot of people's "All-Time Best" lists.

Naturally, you'll have to evaluate these songs based only on their lyrics. But as you read through them, try to imagine an accompaniment of trumpets, harps, lyres, tambourines, stringed instruments, flutes, and even clashing cymbals. (All these instruments are listed in Psalm 150. And where appropriate, this musical worship was accompanied by dancing [150:4].) So don't equate Old Testament music with old fogey music. It had as much life and energy as anything you'll hear on a top-40 station today.

Number Ten
Read Psalm 27:1-14.
Number Ten on our Golden Oldies list is Psalm 27, one penned by David. What did David have to sing about? (27:1-3)

What things did David request in his song? (27:4-9)

What encouragement did David give the listener? (27:13)

What advice did David offer the listener? (27:14)

Number Nine
Read Psalm 121:1-8.
You can see how Psalm 27 is kind of a personal song—much like a soloist might sing today. As we move on to Number Nine on our hit parade, we get to a song geared more for groups. Psalms 120 through 134 are a collection of tunes known as Songs of Ascent. It is thought that as Israelites made annual journeys to Jerusalem, they would sing this group of songs. (Since Jerusalem is at a high altitude, the travelers would have to "ascend" to get there, thus the name, "Songs of Ascent.")

We're going to focus on Psalm 121. But all of these psalms are short, in case you want to go through additional ones on your own. What caused the writer of Psalm 121 to think of God? (121:1)

What assurance did the writer have in receiving help from God? (121:2)

What kind of protection does God offer His people? (121:3-8)

When can you expect God's protection? (121:8)

If you were a traveler on a long pilgrimage to Jerusalem, how do you think this song would have made you feel?

Number Eight
Read Psalm 139:1-24.
Next on our list of greatest hits is Psalm 139, another song by David. The great attraction of this psalm is the description of the relationship between God and the people He created. According to David, exactly *what* does God know about you? (139:1-6)

Where are some of the places God looks after you? (139:7-12)

When did God begin His concern for you? (139:13-16)

Because of God's intense love for David, how did David feel about God's enemies? (139:17-22)

David wanted to be as close to God as possible, so what request did he make of God? (139:23-24)

Getting Personal – *How close do you feel to God after reading this psalm?*

Number Seven
Read Psalm 63:1-11.
But David didn't only look to God during good times. He consistently sought God, even in times of trouble. Our Number Seven song, Psalm 63, was written by David when he was in the desert, being pursued by his enemies. What indication does he give that he was in a desert setting? (63:1)

What sustained David when he seemed isolated and unable to worship God as he normally did? (63:2, 6)

How did David's difficult situation affect his devotion to God? (63:3-5)

What illustration did David use to symbolize God's protection? (63:7-8)

How convinced was David that God would be fair? (63:9-11)

Number Six
Read Psalm 8:1-9.
We now shift from David seeing the desert through the eyes of a fugitive to David viewing God's universe through eyes of wonder. Our Number Six all-time favorite song is Psalm 8. This song is like a sandwich—its contents fit between the statement of its theme in the first and last verses. What thought did David want to emphasize as he opened and closed the psalm? (8:1, 9)

David noted God's praise originating from a seemingly insignificant place. Where? (8:2)

He also saw reason to praise God as he examined a very significant place. Where? (8:3)

As David viewed the heavens, a question came to his mind. What was it? (8:4)

David couldn't really comprehend why a God who could think and create on a level high enough to create the universe could also think on a level "low" enough to care about human beings. Yet David was assured that God *did* care. What made David so sure? (8:5-8)

Getting Personal — *What are some reasons that you are sure that God cares about you?*

Number Five
Read Psalm 119:1-176.
As we move into the top half of our Golden Oldies, we come to Psalm 119. This psalm is noteworthy for several reasons. First, it's the longest psalm. Second, this psalm is an acrostic poem. Each 8 verses compose a stanza, and each stanza begins with a different letter of the Hebrew alphabet. But the main reason we want to single out this psalm is its topic: the benefits provided by the Word of God. Almost every one of the psalm's 176 verses makes a direct reference to God's Word. Take a quick look through the psalm, and write down all the different terms you can find that refer to the Word of God.

How did the writer instruct young people to remain pure? (119:9)

And specifically, how did the writer determine to do so? (119:10-11)

Was the writer at all embarrassed to proclaim and obey God's Word? (119:44-47)

In terms of money, what did the writer have to say about God's Word? (119:72)

In terms of food, what did he have to say? (119:103)

What other illustrations did he use to symbolize God's Word? (119:105)

Did the writer determine to obey God's laws because it made him feel good, or because he was convinced that it was the right thing to do? Explain your answer (119:111-112, 163-168).

Number Four
Read Psalm 24:1-10.

All right, music fans. We're up to Number Four on our charts. And filling that slot is Psalm 24, a song with a challenge. The psalm opens with the statement that the earth and everything in it belongs to God, because He created it. But since that's the case, what requirements did David list for coming into the presence of such a great Landlord? (24:3-4)

What do you think David meant?

What term does David use to describe God? (24:7-10)

Number Three
Read Psalm 1:1-6.
Our Number Three psalm is similar in content to Psalm 24, so turn to Psalm 1 and sing along. The author of this song is unknown, yet the psalm was chosen (appropriately) to lead off the hymnal. Read through the psalm and describe the contrast the author is making.

What are the benefits received by those who follow God wholeheartedly?

What end is in store for wicked people?

The positioning of this psalm is significant. You've seen for yourself that a great many of the psalms have to do with the observations of righteous people in regard to wicked ones. So right up front, it is made clear that God will ultimately reward those who follow Him and will punish those who don't.

Number Two
Read Psalm 100:1-5.
Such a great truth should make us thankful, and that leads to our next song. Number Two with a bullet is Psalm 100. The author has been thinking of all the good things God has done for us, so what does he instruct us to do? (100:1)

What attitude should we have as we worship? (100:2)

What should we know about our relationship with God? (100:3)

What should we do with that knowledge? (100:4)

How long will God have such a relationship with us? (100:5)

Number One
Read Psalm 23:1-6.
And now, for the psalm you've all been waiting for. Here's our Number One all-time favorite [TA-DA], Psalm 23. To help us understand why this is the most-loved psalm of so many people, write down all the verbs (action words) you find in it that describe what God does for you.

What are the characteristics of sheep?

How does your previous answer relate to God as our shepherd?

What pleasant scenes are described in this psalm?

What threatening scenes are described?

After reading this psalm, what possible circumstances can you envision that God wouldn't help you get through safely?

Our time is just about up for this musical session of Old Testament Golden Oldies. Stay tuned next session for the literary portion of our show as we hear excerpts from a best-selling book of quotations that's all the rage. But first, here's a word from our author.

JOURNEY INWARD

This is our final session on the Book of Psalms, but you've by no means had a complete tour of all the portions worth reading. Sessions 6 and 7 tried to lead you through some basic themes in the psalms, and this one allowed you to examine several of them from start to finish. In future times of personal Bible study, you need to read through more of the psalms on your own and select your own favorites.

But for now, reconsider what was presented at the first of this session—the **influence of music on your life.** Try to remember how many hours during the past week that you've been exposed to music. Include the times you consciously listen as well as the times music is playing in your surroundings. Write down your *total* number of "musical" hours.

Now, out of the total hours above, break it down into the following categories:

\# of hours of music that honors God (hymns, Christian music, religious classical music, etc.) _____

\# of hours of music that is neutral (neither honors nor dishonors God) _____

\# of hours of music that dishonors God (music with lyrics that don't really promote Christian values) _____

If you're like most people, your amount of God-honoring music is only a small percentage of your total listening time. So to complete this session, try to compose a song of your own that offers praise and thanks to God. It doesn't have to be on the level of a John Lennon/Paul McCartney Beatles' classic, but it *should* be from the heart.

First, work on the lyrics. What do you want to say? To get started, try answering the following five questions:

(1) What are your favorite images of God? (These can be original and/or from the list you made in Session 6.)

(2) What are some specific things God has done for you lately?

(3) What adjectives would you use to describe God?

(4) What are some good reasons to praise God?

(5) What are some of your unanswered questions or unsolved problems?

Jerusalem Bandstand

Now, using the information you have accumulated, create a psalm of your own. If you wish, make the words fit one of your favorite current songs. But don't feel that you have to put your words to music. Your words don't even have to rhyme. Just be sure they are a sincere expression of praise to God.

Psalm writing can become a good habit if you're willing to work at it. It's a constructive discipline to help you focus on God's attributes and express your praise to Him . So you must do *one* to complete this session, but try another in a week or so if you're up to the challenge. You'll soon discover that *your* songs will probably have a lot more to say than most of the other music you listen to.

KEY VERSE

"Come, let us sing for joy to the Lord; let us shout aloud to the Rock of our salvation. Let us come before Him with thanksgiving and extol Him with music and song" (Psalm 95:1-2).

Everyone seems to be looking for advice.

9

ARE YOU A WISE GUY OR JUST A SMART ALECK?
(Assorted sections of Proverbs)

Dear Ernie,
I am a henpecked husband with a problem. My wife wants me to act like a "mature adult." She doesn't understand when I don't act perfect around her friends. Shouldn't I have a right to just be myself?
Sign me,
Hacked off in Hackensack

Dear Ernie,
I'm a Christian, but people don't treat me like one. You see, every once in a while I have a beer with my non-Christian friends. My Christian "friends" don't like it and avoid me like the plague. If they can't handle it, why should I suffer? Or are they right?
Depressed in Des Moines

Dear Ernie,
 I'm single and I like to date a lot of guys, but everyone says I'm just a flirt. I don't want a serious relationship at this point in my life. Is it wrong for a girl to see a lot of guys? (My closest friends say the word's beginning to spread that I'm "easy," but I'm not!) I need your advice.
Not Easy and Not Happy

No doubt you've seen letters in advice columns similar to the ones you just read. Everyone seems to be looking for advice. (And even when *you're* not looking, it's fun to see what problems *other* people are having.) Most problems don't have easy answers. If they did, they wouldn't be problems, would they? But problems *do* have solutions. And people could avoid a lot of worrying about their problems if they possessed one thing. But this special thing is very rare these days. What is this secret commodity that few people seem to possess, but that can change everyone's life for the better? WISDOM!

JOURNEY ONWARD

You'll remember that wisdom is the one thing that Solomon asked for, when given the opportunity to ask for anything (including riches and fame). And because wisdom was a priority for him, he received riches and fame as well. Yet few people today truly seek wisdom. Oh sure, they would *like* to be smarter. But when it comes to *working* for wisdom or making hard choices that would result in wisdom (rather than fame, riches, and so forth), many people fall short.

The writers of Proverbs (Solomon and others) had much to say about the pursuit of wisdom. They knew that the acquisition of wisdom could help people deal with problems like sex, drinking, popularity, and whatever. The next session will cover a lot of what they had to say about those *specific* problems, but first we want to discuss wisdom in *general* terms.

Read Proverbs 1:1-33.
In fact, one of the main reasons for writing the Book of Proverbs was for "attaining wisdom and discipline" (1:2). What benefits does the author link with attaining wisdom? (1:3-6)

Where should you begin as you look for knowledge and wisdom? (1:7)

But hardly does the author begin to describe the benefits of wisdom than he began to warn of obstacles that get in the way of finding wisdom. How can people get sidetracked in their quest for wisdom? (1:10-14)

Getting Personal – *What obstacles have prevented you from seeking wisdom?*

What happens to those people who refuse to seek wisdom? (1:15-19)

The illustration given in Proverbs 1:17 is a good one. The author suggests that no bird is stupid enough to go flying into a net that it can see is set up to trap him. Yet people who pursue evil rather than wisdom fall into a trap they *should* be able to see. There is no substitute for (nor shortcut to) wisdom.

Next the author personifies wisdom. In other words, he assigns to wisdom the mannerisms and personality traits of a person. He describes a "woman" (Wisdom) roaming the streets and crying out. What is her basic message to those who reject her? (1:20-33)

What is the message to those who choose to honor wisdom? (1:23, 33)

Worth Your While
Read Proverbs 2:1-22.
As soon as the author warns of the obstacles to wisdom, he returns to the benefits. What is one major benefit of wisdom? (2:5)

But what things must be done before that benefit of wisdom can be obtained? (2:1-4)

What is the source of wisdom? (2:6-8)

What are some more benefits of wisdom? (2:9-22)

Read Proverbs 3:1-35.
What are some things you can do to be sure that you hold on to wisdom? (3:1-12)

Exactly how valuable is wisdom? (3:13-15)

Getting Personal – *How much do you value wisdom?*

And there are still more benefits that come with wisdom. What are they? (3:16-18)

Another reason we should seek wisdom is because it is one of God's characteristics. If our goal is to be more like God (which it *should* be), we need to grow wiser as we get older. What was one thing God was able to do through His wisdom? (3:19-20)

Wisdom should influence your life in a number of ways. What difference can wisdom make in each of the following areas?

❑ Your peace of mind (3:21-26)

❑ Your treatment of other people (3:27-30)

❑ Your relationship with God (3:31-35)

Skim Proverbs 4:1-27.
It's never too soon to begin your search for wisdom. The author of Proverbs speaks of being "a boy in my father's house, still tender," when his father challenged him to get wisdom and understanding (4:3-5). He was taught that wisdom was supreme and that it should be acquired at any cost (4:7). Wisdom, when applied, will influence health (4:22-23), speech (4:24), and other activities (4:25-27).

The Flip Side
Read Proverbs 6:1-35.
After repeatedly stressing the need to acquire wisdom, the author shifts his perspective. He begins to teach of some of the results of *not* finding wisdom. Proverbs 5 will be covered in the next session. But Proverbs 6 lists a number of problems people can expect if they decide to pursue foolishness instead of wisdom. One such problem is blindly standing up for someone else without considering the consequences (making promises, cosigning a loan, etc.). It's not a wise thing to do. The author compares it to an animal trapped in a hunter's snare. How should this situation be handled? (6:1-5)

Another unwise habit is laziness. What does the writer challenge lazy people to do? (6:6-8)

What is the eventual outcome of laziness? (6:9-11)

Getting Personal — *On a scale of 1 to 10 with 1 being low and 10 being high, how lazy do you consider yourself? Why?*

A third foolish habit described in this section is troublemaking. Some people become mischief-makers at a young age in order to get attention, look cute, or whatever. But if this becomes a lifestyle for them, what can they expect? (6:12-15)

In Proverbs 6:16-19, you'll find a list of seven things that God hates. List them in the left column of the following chart. In the right column, try to think of an example for each one from your own life or your relationships with other people. You may not think of an example for each of the seven things on the list, but come up with as many as you can.

THINGS GOD HATES	EXAMPLES FROM LIFE
1.	
2.	

THINGS GOD HATES	EXAMPLES FROM LIFE
3.	
4.	
5.	
6.	
7.	

It seems that the writer can't say enough good things about wisdom, and that fact in itself seems to prove how wise he really is. Think about it. If he wants to convince foolish people to become wise, he can't just express his opinion once and expect them to change. These aren't Albert Einsteins he's working with. They need lots of repetition of new ideas before the ideas sink in.

Add to that thought the fact that no one surpassed Solomon (one of the major writers of Proverbs) in the area of wisdom (1 Kings 4:30-31). He was known all over the world because of his knowledge and perception (1 Kings 4:34). So the topic of wisdom was important to Solomon. It had made a major difference in his life, and he wanted his sons (and others) to work hard to acquire wisdom.

Skim Proverbs 7:1–8:36.
Consequently, in Proverbs 8 you will see a lot of the same material you've covered in the previous chapters. The author again personifies wisdom by giving it the personality traits of a woman. (You probably remember that

Solomon knew a lot about women too. If not, review 1 Kings 11:3.) This time, however, he's setting up a comparison between this woman (Wisdom) and a second woman he will introduce in Proverbs 9.

As the woman, Wisdom, makes her speech, she demands the attention of those within earshot. And she makes some good observations. For example, what connections can be found between wisdom and truth? (Proverbs 8:6-9)

Who is Wisdom's roommate? (8:12) [If you aren't sure of the definition of this answer, be sure to look it up.]

What kinds of influence does Wisdom have on people? (8:14-21)

We said before that wisdom is one of God's characteristics. What are some specific ways that God has used wisdom? (8:22-31)

Bachelorette No. 1
Read Proverbs 9:1-18.
Finally, before you finish the Bible study portion of this session, you have the opportunity to play a miniversion of "The Dating Game." Two women are described in Proverbs 9. (You girls will have to imagine the same characteristics assigned to guys.) Read through the description of the first person, make some notes below, and then do the same for the second person. Which person would you rather spend time with?
- ❑ Person #1—WISDOM
    (Proverbs 9:1-12)

Are You a Wise Guy or Just a Smart Aleck?

❏ Person #2—**FOLLY** (FOOLISHNESS)
  (Proverbs 9:13-18)

When the concepts of wisdom and foolishness are personified (made to sound human), there is little doubt as to which is the better choice. Wisdom offers life, food, and learning. Folly offers ignorance, self-indulgence, and death. So why don't more people try harder to gather wisdom? One major reason is that they rarely think ahead to the consequences of their actions. They find out too late that they must pay for all their acts of foolishness. What other reasons can you think of that prevent people—especially young people—from finding wisdom?

JOURNEY INWARD

This session has been very general. Several specific *applications* of wisdom will be dealt with in the next session. But hopefully you've seen that **finding and holding on to wisdom** should be a top priority if you want to achieve success in life.

So let's see how wise you are. Try this simple quiz.

1. Who was the 13th president of the United States?

2. What is the official language of Albania?

3. If line A is 4 inches, line B is 3 inches, and angle AB is a right angle, how long is line C?

4. Who wrote *The House of the Seven Gables?*

5. What common English word contains three consecutive pairs of double letters?

6. Who was the first man to set foot on the moon?

7. What does the Latin phrase *caveat emptor* mean?

8. What is the largest animal ever to have lived?

9. What biblical character fell asleep during a long sermon and fell off a three-story window ledge?

10. What is the official name of the bone more commonly known as your kneecap?

You may be saying, "This is no fair! What does this quiz have to do with the kind of wisdom we've been examining in this session?" If so, your complaints are valid.

The quiz you just took has nothing to do with wisdom. Even if you got all 10 answers right, it would be no proof that you are wise. You would be *knowledgeable*, sure, but there's more to wisdom than comprehending and retaining facts. The wisdom described in Proverbs is *applied* knowledge—your store of facts and figures that are put into practice in some manner. So someone with an IQ slightly higher than a turnip who applies everything he knows can be wiser than a genius who never puts his knowledge into action to make his life better.

The goal of Proverbs is not to develop an army of brainoids who can do calculus without a calculator. Rather, the goal is to challenge each of us to use our knowledge in order to understand more about God and our relationship to Him and His world. Wisdom will never come automatically. It's a hard characteristic to acquire, and it's a lifetime pursuit. Even Solomon with all his wisdom failed late in his life because he stopped applying what he knew to be true. You don't have to make the same mistake.

Oh, yeah. Here are the quiz answers—just so you can be sure you got them all correct: (1) Millard Fillmore; (2) Albanian; (3) 5 inches; (4) Nathaniel Hawthorne; (5) Bookkeeper; (6) Neil Armstrong; (7) "Let the buyer beware"; (8) The whale—larger even than prehistoric dinosaurs; (9) Eutychus—Acts 20:7-12; (10) Patella.

Below are some additional verses about wisdom from Proverbs. During the next week, as you feel yourself slipping in your quest for wisdom, look up one or more of them for a "booster shot" concerning wisdom.

16:16	19:10-11	24:3-7
16:22	19:20-21	24:13-14
17:12	21:30	26:6-12
19:2		

KEY VERSE

"The fear of the Lord is the beginning of wisdom, and knowledge of the Holy One is understanding" (Proverbs 9:10).

You were lucky to land this position at the fortune cookie factory.

10

THE WISE HAVE IT
(Portions of Proverbs)

It's the first day at your new job. And boy, were you lucky to land this one because there aren't many more like it. A position opened up at the fortune cookie factory for someone to write those catchy little sayings that go inside the cookies.

The person who had the job before you was encouraged to take early retirement. He was going up to strangers on the street and greeting them with statements like, "Success in business and much prosperity in your future." "Close encounter with dark-haired stranger." And, "He who laughs last probably didn't get joke." The guy is resting in a nice home now and hopes to be off his medication soon.

Your first assignment is to finish the fortunes your predecessor began. So complete each of the following opening statements with a phrase that will show your new boss how wise and creative you are.

❑ A wife of noble character is her husband's crown, but a disgraceful wife is like...

❑ Better to be a nobody and yet have a servant than...

- ❏ A heart at peace gives life to the body, but envy...

- ❏ Better is a meal of vegetables where there is love than...

- ❏ Do not speak to a fool because...

- ❏ Who has woe? Who has sorrow? Who has strife? Who has complaints? Who has needless bruises? Who has bloodshot eyes? Those who...

- ❏ An honest answer is like...

- ❏ A word aptly spoken is like...

- ❏ If you find honey, eat just enough—too much of it, and...

- ❏ If a man loudly blesses his neighbor early in the morning...

The Wise Have It

❏ A quarrelsome wife is like...

How were your answers? Do you think they're good enough to keep your job? Maybe you've already figured out that your predecessor was borrowing from the Book of Proverbs. So you might want to look up Proverbs 12:4; 12:9; 14:30; 15:17; 23:9; 23:29-35; 24:26; 25:11; 25:16-17; 27:14; and 27:15. You'll see the biblical version of each of the previous statements. And even if you don't think your answers were as good, you probably came up with some wise responses of your own.

JOURNEY ONWARD

In the last session, you saw that the Book of Proverbs has a lot to say about the topic of wisdom. In this session, you'll see how wisdom should be applied to a lot of different areas of life. And in spite of our fortune cookie opening, the wisdom in the Proverbs is much more than cute, catchy sayings. It is a collection of observations about life as recorded by some of the smartest people who ever lived.

One caution should be made at this point. The Proverbs should be put into practice along with some common sense. They are more like guidelines than commands. To illustrate, consider Proverbs 26:4—"Do not answer a fool according to his folly, or you will be like him yourself." It makes sense not to bring yourself down to a foolish person's level and argue back and forth. Right? Right!

Now look at the very next verse, Proverbs 26:5—"Answer a fool according to his folly, or he will be wise in his own eyes." There are times, naturally, when you need to point out the foolishness of someone's argument in order to get to the truth. Right? Right again! As you can see, the proper course of action depends on the situation. It's not enough to have the wisdom to know *what* to do if you don't also have the wisdom to know *when* to do it.

So with this in mind, let's look at some specific areas of life and see what the authors of Proverbs have to tell us about each one.

Area #1— MORAL DEVELOPMENT

According to Proverbs 25:28, a person without self-control is like a city whose walls are broken down—defenseless against any opposition from enemies. And the Book of Proverbs is filled with other instructions concerning honesty, integrity, discipline, and so forth. Why are these characteristics important? (10:9; 11:20-21; 14:12; 15:10; 16:18; 20:30; 22:26-27)

What are some of the benefits of developing a disciplined life? (10:27; 11:1, 3, 5-8; 12:21; 13:18; 14:32; 15:33; 16:32; 19:18-19; 22:4)

When should you start to develop a disciplined life? (22:6, 15)

What are some characteristics of a moral, disciplined life? (24:15-20)

Getting Personal – *How disciplined is your life?*

Area #2 — PERSONAL RELATIONSHIPS

In what specific ways can your friends affect your life? (12:26; 15:22; 16:28-30; 18:24; 27:6, 10, 17)

What kind of family relationships should you strive to develop? (11:29; 13:1; 17:21; 20:20)

What are some practical ways to strengthen your personal relationships? (12:16-17; 13:10; 14:21; 15:30; 17:17; 27:14)

How do you develop a good personal relationship with God? (16:3)

Getting Personal – *How would you rate your relationship with God?*

What illustrations are given for people who misuse personal relationships? (26:17-19)

Area #3 — SPEECH

If you're like most people, your mouth gets a pretty good workout every day. And apparently the people of the Old Testament did their fair share of ear-bending as well. Otherwise there wouldn't have been so much written about the subject. What does the Book of Proverbs have to say about:

❏ Talking too much? (10:10, 19; 17:27-28)

- ❏ Lying? (10:18; 12:22; 24:24-25; 25:18; 26:24-28)

- ❏ Gossip? (20:19; 26:20-22)

- ❏ Boasting? (27:1-2; 30:32-33)

- ❏ Talking before you think about what you're saying? (12:18; 13:3; 20:25)

- ❏ Mocking? (17:5; 22:10)

- ❏ Listening? (18:17)

- ❏ Cursing? (26:2)

- ❏ Flattery? (28:23)

❑ Quarreling? (17:14)

❑ Other sinful talk? (12:13; 14:3)

❑ Proper speech? (10:20; 12:25; 13:14; 15:1, 23; 16:24; 20:15; 22:11; 24:26; 25:11-12, 15)

Getting Personal – *Which area of speech do you struggle with most?*

Area #4 — WORK
We all know that laziness is a bad habit, but perhaps we don't seriously consider the consequences that result when laziness becomes a lifestyle. What are some of the end results of laziness? (10:4-5, 26; 12:24; 18:9; 19:15; 20:4; 21:25-26)

What are a couple of motivations to be a good worker? (11:18; 16:26)

What is the most extreme example of laziness you can think of? When you come up with an answer, compare yours with the examples given in Proverbs 26:14-15.

How can you learn from someone else's laziness? (24:30-34)

Laziness isn't the only thing that prevents people from working productively. What's another? (28:19)

Getting Personal – *How productive a worker are you?*

Area #5 — MONEY AND WEALTH
This category is closely related to the previous one. If you avoid laziness and are a good worker, you aren't likely to have severe money problems. But there's much more to learn about money than how to get lots of it. Your attitude toward money is also very important. What kind of attitude should you develop toward money? (11:24-28)

What can happen to people who think only of themselves? (21:13)

What problems can being rich (or wanting to be rich) bring you? (13:8; 15:27)

What would the author think about some of today's get-rich-quick schemes? (13:11)

Why is a little sometimes better than a lot? (15:16-17)

What's better than being rich? (22:1)

What do rich and poor people have in common? (22:2; 29:13)

To what extent should you focus on wealth? (23:1-5)

Getting Personal – *How much time do you spend daily focused on money?*

Area #6 — DRINKING
How are alcoholic beverages described? (20:1)

What is the connection between wisdom and drinking? (20:1)

What is the connection between wealth and drinking? (23:19-21)

What is the connection between drinking and personal satisfaction with life? (31:4-7)

What are other symptoms and results of drinking? (23:29-35)

Getting Personal – *What decisions have you made in regard to alcohol?*

Area #7 — SEX
Sex is a wonderful gift of God, but it is essential to use it only in proper contexts. The Bible never condemns sex. But it *does* condemn sex outside of the marriage bond—both prior to and outside of marriage. What illustration is used to describe someone who isn't picky about whom he or she fools around with? (11:22)

To what is a prostitute compared? (23:26-28)

The writers of Proverbs had much to say about the topic of sex. Chapters 5–7 are full of warnings concerning any kind of contact with prostitutes. This particular author admits that sure, sometimes illicit sex *looks* good and those people trying to seduce you *sound* good. But why should you make sure you aren't taken in by them? (5:1-6)

The Wise Have It

What is in store for people who practice casual sex? (5:7-14)

What's the best reason to avoid sex outside of marriage? (5:21-23)

Things haven't changed too much since Proverbs was written. While many people are saying "Don't," most of us can expect to encounter people who say, "Do!" God says not to have sex outside of marriage. But there are other good reasons not to. Read Proverbs 6:20-32 and list some of those practical reasons.

Getting Personal – *Has the increase in AIDS-related deaths affected your decisions regarding sex? How?*

Now read Proverbs 7:6-23, which is an eyewitness account by someone observing a prostitute picking up a young man.

❑ Why does he allow her to seduce him?

❑ How does she seduce him?

❑ What is the guy compared to as he gives in to the prostitute?

How can you avoid giving in to the temptation to have sex outside of marriage? (7:1-5)

Area #8 — ATTITUDES TOWARD WOMEN

Much has been written during the past decade to promote women's rights. Magazines have been started, legislation has been passed, and bras have been burned. But long before all such commotion, the Book of Proverbs was around to present a model picture of a "modern" woman. Read Proverbs 31:10-31 and list all the positive qualities you can find about the woman described there.

Now, on the list you just made, put a check mark beside those qualities that the media use to describe a "modern" woman.

JOURNEY INWARD

This session may seem like a potpourri of random topics, but they have a common theme. Each of the areas discussed is just one element of **building a lifestyle based on wisdom.** The lessons learned about wisdom in the last session must be applied to every aspect of life if you are to see results. So think through each of the areas we've covered in this session, and try to evaluate how much wisdom you are showing in each area. Remember: wisdom is *applied* knowledge. So don't evaluate how much you *know*. Determine how well you *practice* what you know.

On the scales below, circle the appropriate number to indicate the amount of wisdom you display.

Area #1—MORAL DEVELOPMENT

Dishonest/   1—2—3—4—5—6—7—8—9—10 Always honest
immoral   and moral

What do you need to do to bring your score up in this area?

Area #2—PERSONAL RELATIONSHIPS

Use or abuse   1—2—3—4—5—6—7—8—9—10   Sensitive and
other people   giving

What do you need to do to bring your score up in this area?

Area #3—SPEECH

Potty   1—2—3—4—5—6—7—8—9—10   Silver
Mouth   tongue

What do you need to do to bring your score up in this area?

Area #4—WORK

Lazy Bum   1—2—3—4—5—6—7—8—9—10   Employee of
                                                                                       the Month

What do you need to do to bring your score up in this area?

Area #5—MONEY AND WEALTH

Greedy   1—2—3—4—5—6—7—8—9—10   Not at all
Money-   concerned
grubber   with money

What do you need to do to bring your score up in this area?

Area #6—DRINKING

Heavy   1—2—3—4—5—6—7—8—9—10   Not even
Drinker   a desire
                                                                     to drink

What do you need to do to bring your score up in this area?

Area #7—SEX

Lustful and   1—2—3—4—5—6—7—8—9—10 Pure thoughts
Looking   and innocent
                                                                         hands

What do you need to do to bring your score up in this area?

Area #8—ATTITUDES TOWARD WOMEN

Sexist ;   1—2—3—4—5—6—7—8—9—10   Total
(if male)   respect
Crazed   for the
Feminist   opposite
(if female)   gender

What do you need to do to bring your score up in this area?

Your challenge for the next week is to take your own advice. Go through your list of comments regarding ways to bring up your scores and actually *do* several of those things. It will be worth the effort. If you don't think so, the next session should give you some motivation to help you change your attitude.

KEY VERSES

"Trust in the Lord with all your heart and lean not on your own understanding; in all your ways acknowledge Him, and He will make your paths straight" (Proverbs 3:5-6).

Ever had a day where you were completely, terminally bored?

11

SATISFACTION ISN'T GUARANTEED

(Book of Ecclesiastes)

Have you ever had one of those days? A day when you are so completely, terminally bored that there's *nothing* you can do about it? Everything on TV is a rerun. You try the radio and the same old songs are playing. You go see your best friend and he (or she) is even more bored than you are. You have no money for shopping. You don't feel like reading. It's too hot for tennis. And the pool's closed for repairs. There is *not a thing* to do.

At such times, you may begin to ask yourself probing questions: "What is the meaning of life?" "Why am I here?" "Is life just a repetition of the same old things over and over and over again?" And, "Why isn't there anything new to do under the sun?"

If you've never felt this way, you probably will one of these days. Most people go through periods of boredom, depression, low energy, or similar emotional conditions. And many assume that all they need to relieve their negative feelings is something new or different—more money, a shopping spree, a vacation, a day at the beach, etc. Sometimes that's all it takes to bust the blues. But other times the problem may be deeper. If someone has gradually developed a general dissatisfaction with life, there may be little if anything that can cheer up that person.

JOURNEY ONWARD

Read Ecclesiastes 1:1-18.

This session takes us into the Book of Ecclesiastes, a book that most people think was written by Solomon. And you probably remember that Solomon was the man who had just about anything he could ask or wish for. He had wisdom, women, riches, fame, glory, the highest position in the kingdom (and the world), and more. It's hard for us to imagine the high standard of living he must have been accustomed to. But as he begins his writing, what does his attitude seem to be concerning the things around him? (Ecclesiastes 1:1-2)

As you go through this book, you'll find the word *meaningless* many times. (Translations other than the *New International Version* use the terms *vanity, emptiness, futility*, or some other equivalent.) However the Hebrew word is translated, it seems that in spite of all the wonderful things that Solomon possessed, he was growing dissatisfied with the quality of his life. Review Ecclesiastes 1:3-11 and make a list of some of his specific complaints.

Getting Personal — *Are you satisfied with your life? Why or why not?*

Having made his general observations, Solomon turns his thoughts to some specific areas of life. The first is wisdom. And it seems strange at first that the person who placed so much emphasis on wisdom in the Book of Proverbs doesn't seem to value it much in Ecclesiastes. But what he's referring to here is a merely human level of wisdom—not the wisdom God provides. (You'll discover this for yourself later, but you need to keep this fact in mind to avoid possible confusion.) What did Solomon think about human wisdom? (1:12-18)

Satisfaction Isn't Guaranteed

Read Ecclesiastes 2:1-26.
Yet even though Solomon was having trouble appreciating wisdom, he still had to admit it was better than something else. What? (2:12-14)

What was really bothering Solomon about wisdom? (2:15-16)

After Solomon failed to find satisfaction in wisdom, he thought he would try pleasure. When *you're* looking for a fun time, you might go out for pizza, rent a video, or play golf. But Solomon's definition of pleasure might not be quite the same as yours. What things did Solomon do in his quest for pleasure? (2:1-10)

Getting Personal – *What things have you pursued in your quest for pleasure?*

What effect did all these pleasures have on Solomon's level of personal satisfaction? (2:11)

Solomon had put a lot of energy and effort into achieving success for his life. So after wisdom and pleasure didn't lead to satisfaction, he thought hard work might do the trick. Was he right? Why or why not? (2:17-23)

And then, after all his musings, Solomon arrives at a key thought—one that he will keep coming back to in this book. What did he discover to be the secret to satisfaction in life? (2:24-26)

If you didn't read that last passage carefully (2:24-26), you may be confused now. You might be thinking that Solomon first said he couldn't find satisfaction in work or in pleasure, but now he is saying that man can do nothing better than to eat, drink, and find satisfaction with work! Isn't that a contradiction? It is until you note the comparison he makes. He says that *God* is the source of wisdom, knowledge, and happiness, and He gives these things to whomever pleases Him (follows Him willingly). The person who obeys God can find great satisfaction with life—in work, pleasure, knowledge, or whatever. But as soon as someone begins to leave God out of the picture, all such activities can become dull, boring, meaningless routines.

A Time for Everything
Read Ecclesiastes 3:1-22.
Then Solomon gets to the best-known section of Ecclesiastes. Reread 3:1-8 and explain why you think Solomon wrote this section at this specific point in his search. (There's no right or wrong answer. Just give your opinion.)

Immediately after writing the section you just read, Solomon repeats what he said previously about finding satisfaction. But this time he gives us another clue as to why it may be hard for people to be satisfied with life on earth. Why? (3:9-14—HINT: The answer has something to do with the word *eternity*.)

Solomon also came to the conclusion that when people don't consider God's influence on their lives, they aren't all that different from other creatures on the earth. Why not? (3:18-21)

But when man's relationship to God is brought to mind, how does mankind differ from all the other creatures? (3:17)

Skim Ecclesiastes 4:1–6:12.
As Solomon observed life on earth, he saw a lot of oppression, some so bad that people would probably look forward to death or wish they had never

been born (4:1-4). But he also noted a way to combat oppression. How? (4:9-12)

Another riddle of Solomon: When is a poor kid better off than a rich king? (4:13)

After still more consideration, Solomon thought of yet another way to maintain a level of satisfaction with life. What things does he suggest? (5:1-7)

What effect does money have on satisfaction with life? (5:8-17)

Is it sinful to have money? Explain your answer (5:18-20).

Getting Personal — *How would you describe your attitude toward money?*

Ecclesiastes 5:19 is a verse that lends support to the "satisfaction isn't guaranteed" theme of this session. If someone tries to enjoy all his possessions just because he has them (without any regard for God's supply), what feelings will he be likely to experience? (6:1-9)

Back to Wisdom
Read Ecclesiastes 7:1-29.
It seems as if it's hard for Solomon to write or speak too long without coming back to the subject of wisdom. He first observes that people are more prone to become wise during their times of distress than during joyful times (7:1-6). He then points out that wisdom is both a shelter that preserves life (7:12)

and a source of power (7:19). He also lists some things that wise people won't do. What are they?

❑ 7:9

❑ 7:10

❑ 7:16

❑ 7:17

❑ 7:21-22

As Solomon observed human beings, what percentage of them did he find to be wise and upright? (7:27-29)

Read Ecclesiastes 8:1-17.
Wisdom is closely related to obedience. Read Solomon's instructions for getting along well with kings, and explain how you can use the same advice to get along better with others (8:2-6).

Should wrongdoers be smug if they get by with some sin without getting punished? Why or why not? (8:11-13)

Solomon realized that he could expect to find certain injustices in people's lives on earth. How did he let that fact influence his ultimate satisfaction with life? (8:14-15)

Read Ecclesiastes 9:1-18.
He also realized that no matter how good or bad people are, eventually they all are going to die. But he came to the logical conclusion that life is much better than death. What was the reasoning he gave to support his pro-life stance, even though he still felt that much of life was meaningless? (9:3-10)

Is a swift, strong, wise, brilliant, knowledgeable person assured of success? Why? (9:11)

What other injustice was observed by Solomon? (9:13-16)

Getting Personal – *What injustices do you see in the world today?*

Skim Ecclesiastes 10:1–11:10.
Chapters 10 and 11 of Ecclesiastes contain further observations by Solomon. Skim these two chapters and select the three verses that best reflect the way you feel about life right now.

Read Ecclesiastes 12:1-14.
Ecclesiastes 12:1-8 contains another graphic reminder that we all are going to die one of these days. Since death is so certain and since judgment is sure (11:9), what's the best step a young person can take to have a healthy attitude toward life? (12:1)

Only by taking this step can you avoid the eventual conclusion that everything is meaningless (12:8) or a chasing after the wind (1:14).

After all of Solomon's heavy thoughts and mental debates, what was his final conclusion concerning life on earth? (12:13-14)

JOURNEY INWARD

Do you ever feel like Solomon did when he wrote Ecclesiastes? Hopefully not. Even during your most severe bouts with boredom, you may not be as frustrated as Solomon seemed to be in his search for meaning. Then again, maybe you are.

If so, the same cure will work for you that worked for Solomon. You can reach the same conclusion that **satisfaction with life** is found by fearing God and keeping His commandments. But first you need to identify your major sources of dissatisfaction. Below are the areas in which Solomon sought meaning.

Assign a percentage to each of these areas to indicate how much you depend on them for meaning. For example, a workaholic may put 65% of his effort into his work, and only 5% in each of the other areas as he seeks fulfillment. Others may rely heavily on friends. Still others may try to pamper themselves with pleasures. Whatever you determine, your total should add up to 100%.

_____	Wisdom	_____	Friends
_____	Pleasures	_____	Money
_____	Work	_____	God
_____	Spouse	_____	Children

After you've assigned percentages to show how much time and energy you spend in each area, go through the same eight categories and evaluate how much satisfaction you receive from each area. Use letter grades to do this (A–, B+, C, etc.).

Satisfaction Isn't Guaranteed

_____ Wisdom   _____ Friends
_____ Pleasures   _____ Money
_____ Work   _____ God
_____ Spouse   _____ Children

Finally, make two evaluations. First compare the percentage answers to your letter grades. This comparison will help make sure you aren't "spinning your wheels," so to speak. For example, if your friends are causing you more grief than comfort (let's say you rated them a C+), yet you go to them 65% of the time when you're seeking satisfaction, then you may have a problem. Make sure the areas that give you greatest satisfaction are the ones on which you focus most of your effort.

Second, it is possible to have straight A's in your letter grades—if you practice what Solomon is preaching. If God is central in your life, He should get an A+. And as a result, you should find a proper balance of pleasures and work, a respect for wisdom, a healthy (non-greedy) attitude toward money, meaningful times with your spouse and children, and a wide circle of friends. Sure, this may not yet have taken place in your life, but it's *possible*.

Let your goal this week be to put God first—no matter what—and see how that decision affects your level of satisfaction with life. The choice is yours: Include God in your life or ignore Him in order to seek fulfillment elsewhere. The second option leads to frustration and an awful feeling that life is meaningless. The first option leads to a life filled with satisfaction. Guaranteed!

KEY VERSE

"Remember your Creator in the days of your youth, before the days of trouble come and the years approach when you will say, 'I find no pleasure in them'" (Ecclesiastes 12:1).

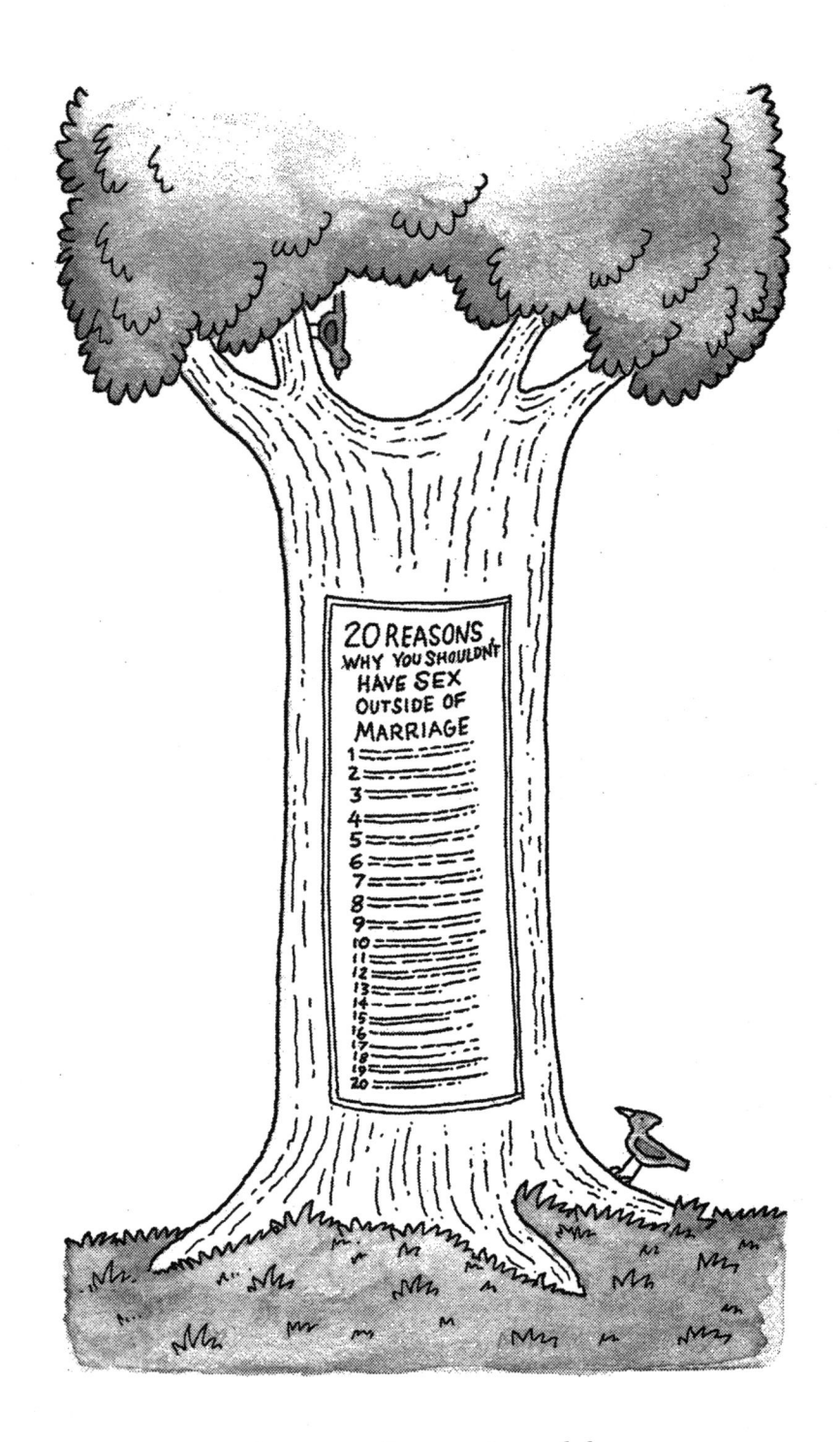

A top-secret document is revealed.

12
JUST AN OLD-FASHIONED LOVE SONG

(Book of Song of Songs)

You probably suspected the following document had to exist somewhere. Your parents probably quoted it to you when you were a teenager. The original must have been carved in a tree in the Garden of Eden—or at least inside one of the great pyramids of Egypt. And married couples, as soon as they discover they are going to become parents, obtain a copy and begin to memorize it so they will be prepared when "the time" comes.

Now, for the first time ever, this top-secret document is being printed for everyone to see. (If it's too much of a shock for your nervous system, you may want to quit reading for a while and catch your breath.) Here goes:

20 REASONS WHY YOU SHOULDN'T HAVE SEX OUTSIDE OF MARRIAGE

1. The Bible says it's wrong.
2. It can ruin your reputation. (Generally considered out-of-date as of the late1960s)
3. It's unacceptable social behavior. (Generally considered out-of-date as of the mid-1970s)
4. The woman can get pregnant.
5. You can get lice.
6. You can get herpes, gonorrhea, and who-knows-what other sexually transmitted diseases.
7. You can die of AIDS or pass it on to your spouse.
8. You might have to get married before you're ready (and most such

marriages don't last).
9. You could get caught in the act, and that would be really embarrassing.
10. Premarital sex will give you a lot of bad mental baggage when you *do* get married.
11. After having sex, the other person may never want to see you again.
12. Premarital sex is the first step toward a life of crime and prostitution.
13. Sex is dirty.
14. Sex degrades the other person.
15. If everybody else jumped off the Empire State Building, would you do it too?
16. Sex is a gift that should be unwrapped only after marriage.
17. Your friends won't respect you after you start having sex.
18. There's a Mr./Miss Right waiting for you.
19. Extramarital sex can have long-term consequences for your marriage, family life, and career.
20. You risk losing relationships, personal belongings, and income if divorce results from extramarital sex.

No doubt you've heard other reasons you could add to the list. And you know that some of these excuses are weak and misguided (#13, for instance). But most of these reasons are valid. Yet statistics tell us that most young adults won't wait till marriage to have sex. The sex drive is strong. When you add peer pressure, the need to be accepted, the negative role models in most movies, feelings of rebellion, and the suggestion by the advertising and print media that sexual activity is perfectly acceptable, not nearly enough people are saying no to extramarital sex.

What more can be said in favor of saving sex for marriage? One thing that's not being said often enough is this: "How much fun can sex be (outside of marriage, that is)?" Granted, sex was created by God to be a real thriller, but the actual act is a tiny proportion of any relationship. Let's say that a sexually active couple averages 14 minutes of passion per day (sexual intercourse after the hand-holding, kissing, caressing, and other acceptable forms of romance). That 14 minutes is less than one percent of the 1,440 minutes in a day.

That leaves more than 99% of the couple's relationship to deal with such questions as: Does (s)he really love me? Has (s)he ever done this with anyone else? I wonder what (s)he is telling other people about me? Is our birth control working? What if I get/she gets pregnant? Do I really believe

Just an Old-Fashioned Love Song

that what we're doing is right? How will I explain this to my husband/wife? And so on.

With all the other major considerations that are involved, how much genuine fun can a sexually-active relationship produce? Is it really worth that less-than-1% of the time spent having sex? Wouldn't the tremendous peace of mind you get from waiting be worth preserving sex for marriage?

Many people who have gotten tangled up in extramarital sex can tell you that romance without sex would have been much preferable to sex without romance. Thousands of young adults each year discover the hard way that sexual activity doesn't always lead to love and romance. However, this session will show that love (and patience) can lead to a marriage relationship, romance (that puts cheap paperbacks to shame), and wonderful sexual activity in its proper context.

JOURNEY ONWARD
Read Song of Songs 1:1-14.
This session will cover Song of Songs (or Song of Solomon). The phrase "song of songs" means "the greatest song" (like Jesus' title, "King of kings" means "the greatest king"). Many people believe Solomon to be the author, though the book could have been written for or about him.

The characters are the woman (also referred to as "bride" or "beloved"), the man (also known as "king," "lover," or "Solomon"), and a group of friends who occasionally comment on what's going on. (If your Bible doesn't contain a breakdown that lets you know what each person is saying, you may want to find one that does. The comments in this session are based on the conversation as divided in the *New International Version*.)

You may never have studied this book of the Bible in Sunday School. It presents a straightforward defense of the joy of romantic love. The images presented aren't crude, but neither do they sidestep the passion of love.

For example, what indications does the woman give right away to suggest that she isn't shy about expressing her feelings of love? (1:2-4)

Getting Personal — *Are you shy about expressing your feelings? Why or why not?*

In Solomon's day, it wasn't the popular trend for women to have dark tans. Light-skinned women were considered more desirable. So why was the woman in this story troubled? (1:5-6)

What did the man think about the woman's appearance? (1:9-11)

Not only did these two like each other's looks; they also liked the smells that brought the other to mind. While they didn't have a vast assortment of expensive colognes to choose from, they *did* have perfume. And the man reminded the woman of what other two natural, pleasant-smelling things? (1:12-14)

Read Song of Songs 1:15–2:2.
Write down any indications that might suggest that the two lovers spent part of their courtship outdoors. (NOTE: The word *verdant* in 1:16 [NIV] means "green with growing plants.")

Read Song of Songs 2:3-17.
What physical effect does love have on the woman? (2:3-5)

What do you think the woman means when she cautions her friends, "Do not arouse or awaken love until it so desires"? (NOTE: She repeats this phrase several times in this book.)

What images come to the woman's mind as she thinks of the man? (2:8-13)

What image comes to the man's mind as he thinks of the woman? (2:14)

How exclusive is the relationship between these two? (2:16)

Read Song of Songs 3:1-11.
How did the woman feel when she wasn't with the man? (3:1-4)

Getting Personal – *How do you feel when you aren't with the people you care about?*

Most likely, Song of Songs 3:6-11 is a description of the wedding party of the bride and groom. Review the passage and write down the things at Solomon's wedding that you didn't (or probably won't) have at yours.

Love Talk
Read Song of Songs 4:1-16.
So far, the woman has been doing most of the talking. But at this point the man opens up. What specific physical features of his bride does he compliment? (4:1-7)

Since you're not from the culture or time period of this couple, you might not feel real flattered to be told that your hair is like a flock of goats and your teeth are like sheep. But most goats of the area were black, and the image the groom had in mind was his bride's long black hair cascading down her neck. He then contrasted her beautiful dark hair with her beautiful white teeth—as bright as sheep that had just been shorn and washed. Even his description of the woman's breasts (4:5) is a gentle, tasteful one—not like the vast assortment of crude descriptions many men use today.

Getting Personal — *What physical features do you notice first about the opposite sex?*

What other objects does the groom use to symbolize his bride's beauty and his love for her? (4:10-15)

Read Song of Songs 5:1-16.
How does the woman feel as she anticipates her groom's arrival at home? (5:2-5)

The woman's friends want to know why she thinks her man is superior to all the other men she might have chosen from (5:9). What does she tell them? (5:10-16)

Read Song of Songs 6:1-13.
Did the groom think other women would be jealous of his bride? Why or why not? (6:8-9)

Read Song of Songs 7:1-13.
You don't have to read too much of Song of Songs to figure out that this couple really enjoyed looking at each other. Most of the man's previous descriptions of the woman focused on the top half of her body. But now review 7:1-5 and notice how his gaze starts at her feet and works its way up to her head. Then reread 7:6-9a and describe what the man wanted to do after seeing how beautiful his bride was.

Just an Old-Fashioned Love Song

What did the woman want to do? (7:9b-13)

Read Song of Songs 8:1-14.
The last chapter of Song of Songs contains a contrast to show how much the woman has matured. Verses 8 and 9 are the words of her brothers as they had looked after her when she was younger. Verses 10-12 are the woman's words at the time of writing. How had time changed the woman's life?

The key to Song of Songs is found in 8:6-7. What did this couple discover about real love that we should remember?

JOURNEY INWARD

In case you haven't noticed yet, Song of Songs is a pretty sensual book to be included in Holy Scripture. It's a lot more interesting to read about **romantic love and sex** than, say, the instructions in Leviticus concerning mildew. (No joke. See Leviticus 13:47-59.) But you should also have noticed that Song of Songs was written tactfully. Even though it recorded intimate details of a romantic/sexual relationship, there was never any hint that the people involved were mere sex objects. Both of them were able to share their innermost thoughts and feelings with the other person.

Did you see the importance of preserving sex for marriage? A person is probably never closer to someone else (and never more vulnerable) than while engaged in sex. The Apostle Paul refers to having sex as "becoming one" with the other person (1 Corinthians 6:15-17). Once it's done, it cannot be reversed. And if the sex act isn't cushioned by the intimacy of marriage, a lot of damage can be done. It's bad enough to share your deep hopes and dreams with someone you care about and discover that the other person doesn't *really* care. Think how much worse it is to have sex with someone and then find yourself rejected.

Preserving sex for marriage is *not* just some dumb out-of-date belief that our parents tried to force upon us as "youngsters." It is a God-ordained command that exists for our own good (and the good of society as well).

If you're not in a dating and/or sexual relationship, ask yourself the following questions:

- ❏ Is the reason that I'm not sexually active because of my Christian convictions, or simply because the right opportunity hasn't come along yet?
- ❏ Where am I going to draw the line with physical contact when I *am* dating?
- ❏ Do I focus on things that put me in a proper frame of mind? (In other words, does church activity and Bible study get equal time with movies, magazines, music, and other things that say sex is OK?)

If you're already married, or in a dating and/or sexual relationship, ask yourself the following questions:

- ❏ Do I need to ask forgiveness (from God, my spouse, or the other person) for previous improper sexual activity?
- ❏ Do I love my spouse (or the other person) enough to preserve sex for marriage?
- ❏ What things can I do from now on to focus more on romance?

These questions are likely to raise others of your own. And you need to think through *all* of them. If you have been sexually active for a while (prior to or during marriage), it may be hard to quit now. But it can be done. Don't hesitate to see a pastor or counselor if you need help getting your sex life straightened out.

Before we leave Song of Songs behind to move on to other things, it should be noted that many people think of it as an allegory for the love between Christ and the church. If you've ever sung the song, "His Banner Over Me Is Love," you'll recognize several of the phrases in this book of the Bible. (For example, see 2:4 and 2:16.) Many such comparisons can be made. But to ignore the Song of Songs other than to illustrate a New Testament spiritual relationship is to miss out on good biblical literature that is found nowhere else. It's important to remind ourselves regularly that God doesn't frown on sex and passion. He just wants us to make sure we don't misuse them. And when you get full control of your sex life, you'll discover that you have something to sing about.

KEY VERSE

"Many waters cannot quench love; rivers cannot wash it away. If one were to give all the wealth of his house for love, it would be utterly scorned" (Song of Songs 8:7).

BEFORE YOU LEAVE

Before you toss this book on your shelf and forget about it, would you take a couple of minutes to fill out the survey on page 179? We value your input on our products as we try to target our materials for your specific needs. Please let us know what you think.

And if you thought this was an OK book, you may want to move on to Book 4 in the **BibleLog Thru the Old Testament** series: *Watchmen Who Wouldn't Quit*. No one will blame you if you're more than a little tired of reading about all the kings of Israel and Judah by now. But the hard part is behind you. Now that you've been through the chronological account of the kings, the next two books will cover the best literature of that era, some of the prophets, and the events after the captivity of Israel and Judah. So don't give up now. You're halfway through the Old Testament series.

GETTING TOGETHER

A Leader's Guide for Small Groups

Before you jump into this leader's guide in all the excitement of preparing for Session 1, take time to read these introductory pages.

Because the basic Bible content of the study is covered inductively in 12 chapters, group members should work through each assigned chapter before attending the small group meeting. This isn't always easy for busy adults, so encourage group members with a phone call or note between some of the meetings. Help them manage their time by pointing out how they can cover a few pages in a few minutes daily, and having them identify a regular time that they can devote to the **BibleLog** study.

Notice that each session is structured to include the following:

- Session Topic—a brief statement of purpose for the session.
- Icebreaker—an activity to help group members get better acquainted with the session topic and/or each other.
- Discussion Questions—a list of questions to encourage group participation.
- Optional Activities—supplemental ideas that will enhance your study.
- Assignment—directions for preparation and suggestions for memorization of key Scriptures.

Here are a few tips that can lead to more effective small group studies:

- Pray for each group member, asking the Lord to help you create an open atmosphere, so that everyone will feel free to share with each other and you.
- Encourage group members to bring their Bibles to each session. This series is based on the *New International Version*, but it is good to have several translations on hand for purposes of comparison.
- Start on time. This is especially important for the first meeting because it will set the pattern for the rest of the course.

- ❑ Begin with prayer, asking the Holy Spirit to open hearts and minds and to give understanding so that Truth will be applied.
- ❑ Involve everyone. As learners, we retain only 10 percent of what we hear, 20 percent of what we see, 65 percent of what we hear and see, *but* 90 percent of what we hear, see, and do.
- ❑ Promote a relaxed environment. Arrange your chairs in a circle or semi-circle. This promotes eye contact among members and encourages more dynamic discussion. Be relaxed in your own attitude and manner.

1

Session Topic: When we repent after our spiritual defeats, God offers us a fresh new start.

Icebreaker
Share with the rest of the group a personal tragedy from your life. Ask: **Did your life fall apart as a result of the tragedy? If so, how did you start over again?**

Discussion Questions
1. How would you describe Ezra's character?
2. How was Ezra's life marked by trust in the Lord?
3. What motivated the Jews to recommit themselves to the Lord and the rebuilding of His temple?
4. What would you identify as the theme of Ezra?

Prayer
Focus on Ezra's prayer in Ezra 9:6-15. Discuss the patterns in this prayer for confession of sin. Write your own prayer of confession patterned after Ezra's example.

Optional Activities
1. Point out that Ezra's life was marked by moral integrity. Discuss which of Ezra's traits you would like to develop in your own life.
2. Spend some time thinking about your spiritual commitment. Ask: **Do you need to be spiritually, morally, or socially restored?** Explain that rebuilding the temple was an affirmation of faith and a measure of spiritual commitment of the Jews. Ask: **What serves as the measure of your spiritual commitment?**

Assignment
1. Complete Session 2.
2. Memorize Ezra 8:22.

2

Session Topic: Pleasing God is more important than receiving praise from others.

Icebreaker
Review the criticisms you listed in the **Journey Inward** section. Try to categorize the criticisms you received in one of the following categories: physical appearance, actions, or speech. Ask: **Which kind of criticism bothers you the most?**

Discussion Questions
1. What was the significance of Nehemiah's role as cupbearer to the king?
2. What role did prayer play in Nehemiah's life?
3. List the problems faced by Nehemiah. How did he overcome each problem?
4. What can you learn from Nehemiah about dealing with problems and making progress toward personal and spiritual goals?
5. What tactics did Nehemiah use to handle criticism?

Prayer
Ask God to help each group member learn to deal more effectively with criticism.

Optional Activities
1. On a map of Jerusalem during the time of Nehemiah, have your group locate the 10 gates and 4 towers mentioned in Nehemiah 3.
2. Divide into small groups to study Nehemiah's prayers in the following passages: 1:4-11; 2:4; 4:9; 6:9.

Assignment
1. Complete Session 3.
2. Memorize Nehemiah 8:10.

3

Session Topic: Every good coincidence is a result of God's perfect timing and intervention.

Icebreakers *(choose one)*
1. Put two columns on a chalkboard or poster paper with the following headings: (1) Symbols of Good Luck and (2) Symbols of Bad Luck. List as many items as possible under each column. Ask: **Do you ever consider yourself lucky?**
2. Write the following words on the chalkboard: *chance, coincidence, fate, fortune, luck.* Ask: **What percentage of close calls, coincidences, or fortunate opportunities are a result of luck? What percentage are a result of God's work in your life?**

Discussion Questions
1. List all the indicators of God's work in Esther's life.
2. Identify Esther's strengths and weaknesses. Which of her strengths and weaknesses do you see in your own life?
3. What is one incident that illustrates how God is in control of the details of your life?
4. How can you praise God for His timing and intervention in your life?

Prayer
Thank God for the way He has (and will continue) to work in your life.

Optional Activities
1. Study Esther's names. Explain that Esther's Hebrew name was *Hadassah* which means "myrtle." Her Persian name *Ester* is derived from the word for "star."
2. Have your group perform "You're in Control, Lord," the reader's theater on page 162.

Assignment
1. Complete Session 4.
2. Memorize Esther 4:16.

YOU'RE IN CONTROL, LORD

All:	Are You in control, Lord?
Esther:	You allowed me to grow up without my real parents. My nation is persecuted by the Persians. Now I've been taken away by the king's attendants to become part of Xerxes' harem.
All:	Are You really in control, Lord?
Mordecai:	You gave me this wonderful cousin who has been like a daughter to me. Now You allow Xerxes to take her away.
All:	Just how much control do You have, Lord?
Esther:	I've found favor with Hegai.
All:	Lord . . . You must have influenced the man.
Mordecai:	But she can't tell anyone that she is a Jew.
All:	It doesn't sound as if You're in control, Lord.
Esther:	God, I've been chosen queen, but some of the king's officers are conspiring to assassinate him.
All:	Now what, Lord?
Mordecai:	Lord, thank You for exposing the plot through Esther.
All:	Lord, we see how You worked through Esther and Mordecai.
Mordecai:	Haman hates me, Lord. My people and I are doomed to death because of his hatred for Jews.
All:	What happened to Your control, Lord?
Esther:	I may die if I enter the king's courts without being summoned. Yet, I must do this if I am to help Mordecai and save my people.
All:	Lord, how will You control this?
Esther:	God, thank You for giving me courage to expose evil Haman. Now I await to see how You will control the problems and difficulties in my life.
Mordecai:	God, thank You for mercy and watchful care over Esther's and my lives.
All:	Yes, God, thank You for being in control of all of our lives.

4

Session Topic: God allows us to go through periods of suffering for the purpose of growth and instruction.

Icebreaker
In small groups, write an answer for one or more of the following questions:
- Why do greedy people prosper while the poor starve?
- Why must some people suffer violent death when disasters hit their homes?
- Why do the "good" die young and the "bad" live long, healthy lives?
- Why are some people born with physical and mental disabilities?
- Why do some people have to go through long periods of pain before death?

Ask: **How do our answers reflect our understanding of God's character? Do we see God as incapable of preventing suffering? As an unseen Force who makes us suffer for no apparent reason? A Father who disciplines us constantly?**

Discussion Questions
1. Why did Job's friends have such a hard time understanding why God permitted him to suffer?
2. How would you describe the attitude of Job's wife toward the suffering she and her husband experienced?
3. List some specific examples of Job's suffering in each of the following areas: physical, emotional, and spiritual.

Prayer
Ask God to give each group member courageous patience to face trials in their lives.

Optional Activities
1. Have the group skim Job 1–27 and write down questions about God, Satan, and suffering. Then divide into smaller groups to explore the answers to the questions.

2. Discuss the fairness of God. Ask: **How can we maintain Job's attitude as expressed in Job 2:10.**

Assignment
1. Complete Session 5.
2. Memorize Job 2:10.

5

Session Topic: God wants us to consider Him our first source of advice.

Icebreaker
Clip some newspaper advice columns, excluding the columnists' answers. Divide the group into several small groups, and have each group offer some advice in their own written responses. Discuss the reliability of the advice given by the groups as well as the newspaper columnists.

Discussion Questions
1. How do you know when advice is reliable?
2. Can anyone really understand God?
3. What sources of advice do you consider most reliable and trustworthy?
4. If you were Job's friend, what advice would your give him about his suffering?

Prayer
Ask God to help group members learn how to serve as godly comforters to people experiencing tragedy.

Optional Activities
1. Ask a counselor to speak to your group about the needs, benefits, and techniques of counseling. Make plans to set up a counseling ministry.
2. Write an imaginary letter from Job's perspective, describing his suffering and asking for advice. Read the letter and ask group members to write a letter of response to Job.

Assignment
1. Complete Session 6.
2. Memorize Job 37:23.

6

Session Topic: Our perceptions of God can be expanded by looking at a variety of descriptions of His character in the Psalms.

Icebreaker
Put the following list of words on a chalkboard. Ask group members to compare their concepts of God with the psalmists' perceptions.

Judge	*Ghost*	*Shepherd*
King	*Father*	*Great Bird*
Light	*Creator*	*Rock*
General	*Lifeguard*	*Record-keeper*
Sun	*Castle*	*Water*

Discussion Questions
1. How has your perspective of God—the Father, Son, and Holy Spirit—increased with your study of the Psalms?
2. How will your new perspective on God affect your life?
3. What quality of God do you appreciate the most?

Prayer
Give thanks and praise to God for the many roles He has in your life.

Optional Activities
1. Plan a worship service based on one or two attributes of God found in the Psalms.
2. Ask a volunteer to prepare a short report on the background, authors, classification, and themes of the Book of Psalms.
3. Point out that there are at least 11 other psalms in the Old Testament in addition to the Book of Psalms. Assign one of the following passages to each group member: Exodus 15:1-18; Deuteronomy 32:1-43; Judges 5; 1 Samuel 2:1-10; 2 Samuel 22:2-51; Job 3; Isaiah 12:4-6; Isaiah 38:9-20;

Lamentations 3:19-38; Jonah 2:1-9; Habakkuk 3:2-19.

Assignment
1. Complete Session 7.
2. Memorize Psalm 27:1.

7

Session Topic: God wants us to develop an open, honest relationship with Him through prayer.

Icebreaker
Ask: **How honest are you with God?** Point out that some Christians are dishonest with God when they refuse to trust Him to love them in spite of their failures. Ask: **How can we develop a more honest relationship with God who loves us more than family and friends who accept us as we are?**

Discussion Questions
1. When was the last time you prayed? What was the occasion?
2. How much time did you spend in prayer this past week?
3. Describe a time when God answered your prayers in an unusual way.
4. Do you have difficulty praying? Why or why not?

Prayer
Pray the key verses for this session, Psalm 139:23-24.

Optional Activities
1. Share four characteristics of dynamic prayer and ask group members to answer the accompanying questions truthfully: Frequency (How often do you pray?); Anticipation (Do you look forward to your prayer time?); Passionate (Do you pray with feeling?); Transformation (How is prayer affecting your life?).
2. Write short prayers that include the following: Praise for God's complex character; Confession of feelings toward God; Thanksgiving for God's identification with our feelings; Requests for faith to share every aspect of our lives within the context of a personal relationship with God.

Assignment
1. Complete Session 8.
2. Memorize Psalm 139:23-24.

8

Session Topic: Listening to music that honors God influences our lives.

Icebreaker
Take the following Music I.Q. Test.
1. How many days did it take for Handel to compose the "Messiah"?
2. How old was Mozart when he wrote his first symphony?
3. What composer is called the "Waltz King"?
4. What city is known as the jazz center of the world?
5. Name the author of the words to "The Star-Spangled Banner."
6. What American composer is called the "March King"?
7. Who is the composer of "White Christmas"?
8. Who was nicknamed the "King of Rock and Roll"?
9. Who is known as the "Queen of Soul"?
10. What female Christian singer from Nashville crossed over from Contemporary Christian music to popular rock music?
11. Identify the "Boss" of Rock and Roll.
12. Name the musical team who wrote "South Pacific" and "Oklahoma."

Answers: 1. 18; 2. 8; 3. Johann Strauss; 4. Chicago; 5. Francis Scott Key; 6. John Philip Sousa; 7. Irving Berlin; 8. Elvis Presley; 9. Aretha Franklin; 10. Amy Grant; 11. Bruce Springsteen; 12. Rodgers and Hammerstein.

Discussion Questions
1. How many hours do you listen to music that honors God? That dishonors God?
2. How much influence does music have on your life?
3. What kind of music has the most influence on your life?
4. How often do you affirm God's worth through the music you sing or listen to?

Prayer
Ask God to help you be more sensitive to music that honors Him.

Optional Activities
1. Invite a professional musician who is a Christian to speak to and perform

for your group. Encourage him to explain his philosophy of how music affects the hearer.
2. Do a study of the Hebrew word *Zamar.* Explain that the word means "to sing praise" or "to make music." Point out that this word suggests the use of musical instruments in praising God.

Assignment
1. Complete Session 9.
2. Memorize Psalm 95:1-2.

9

Session Topic: A wise person gets his wisdom from the Lord and applies that wisdom to specific issues.

Icebreakers (choose one)
1. Describe the wisest person you have ever known.
2. Complete the following sentence: **A wise person is one who....**

Discussion Questions
1. List characteristics of a wise person. Then list characteristics of the most intelligent persons you have known. Discuss the similarities and differences.
2. If you could be intelligent or wise, which quality would you choose? Why?
3. What are some ways to develop a healthy fear and knowledge of the Lord?
4. What one proverb will you put into practice during the next week?

Prayer
Ask God to help each person become more sensitive to the contribution of Proverbs to his or her own life and relationship with God.

Optional Activities
1. Do a word study of *wisdom*. Explain that wisdom comes from the root Hebrew word *hakam* which occurs in the Old Testament over 300 times.
2. Divide into teams to read and illustrate one proverb from each chapter of Proverbs.

Assignment
1. Complete Session 10.
2. Memorize Proverbs 9:10.

10

Session Topic: God wants us to build a lifestyle based on wisdom.

Icebreaker
As group members arrive, offer each person a Chinese fortune cookie. Compare the worldly wisdom of the fortune cookie sayings with the Proverbs you've been studying.

Discussion Questions
1. Discuss the worldly wisdom portrayed below in each lifestyle area.
   - ❏ **Personal Relationships** "What my family and friends don't know won't hurt them."
   - ❏ **Moral Development** "You have to decide whether something is right for you. There are no absolutes."
   - ❏ **Speech** "Swear and they'll know you mean business."
   - ❏ **Work** "Success is being retired at 40."
   - ❏ **Attitudes** "The only thing you can depend on is yourself."
   - ❏ **Drinking** "One beer can't hurt you. Be a party animal."
   - ❏ **Sex** "If you have protection and can handle the consequences, it's OK."
   - ❏ **Money and Wealth** "Money *can* buy happiness."
2. Find a relevant proverb for each of the topics listed above. Summarize that topic as expressed in Proverbs.

Prayer
Ask God to help each person commit himself or herself to practicing the advice and wisdom of Proverbs in each of the eight lifestyle areas.

Optional Activities
1. Research wisdom literature that has been found in other countries of the Near East. Point out that the style of these writings was similar to the Book of Proverbs, but the sayings lacked the righteous standards of God.
2. Notice how the Book of James and the Book of Proverbs are similar. Compare the treatments in each book of the tongue and earthly and divine wisdom.

Assignment
1. Complete Session 11.
2. Memorize Proverbs 3:5-6.

11

Session Topic: Satisfaction with life is found by fearing God and keeping His commandments.

Icebreaker
Ask: Has life ever seemed meaningless to you? Have you ever known anyone who tried to find life's meaning in work, recreational activities, other religions, sexual relationships, or addictive substances? Were they successful?

Discussion Questions
1. How does Solomon's search for meaning in life compare with Job's search after his losses?
2. Why do we need to find a purpose and meaning in life?
3. Brainstorm ways to use significant portions of the Book of Ecclesiastes to help non-Christians understand the futility of knowledge, wealth, and pleasure.

Prayer
Ask God to help each person commit himself or herself to sharing portions of Ecclesiastes with a friend or family member who is depressed or struggling with problems.

Optional Activities
1. Play a recording of Sheila Walsh's "Turn, Turn, Turn" (*Portrait*, Sparrow). Discuss the Scripture this song is based on.
2. Do a study of the word *Elohim* in the Book of Ecclesiastes. Point out that the exclusive use of Elohim (rather than Yahweh) shows that the Creator/creature relationship (rather than the Redeemer/redeemed relationship) is being examined.

Assignment
1. Complete Session 12.
2. Memorize Ecclesiastes 12:1.

12

Session Topic: God wants us to develop a positive view of sex in marriage.

Icebreakers *(choose one)*
1. Have group members read aloud Song of Songs (NIV). Select a male and female to read the roles of "Beloved" and "Lover." The rest of the group can read the "Friends" sections.
2. List characteristics of the relationship between the two lovers. Discuss the following dimensions:
   - attraction
   - sexual longing
   - intimacy
   - friendship
   - joy
   - unity
   - separation
   - loyalty

Discussion Questions
1. Compare the beautiful, but sensual, language of Song of Songs with the graphic language and specific terms for sex organs and sexual activity in today's romantic literature.
2. How do you think God views sex?
3. Why is Song of Songs in the Bible? What does it teach you about romantic love?
4. Where does real love begin?
5. In what context does God affirm sexual intercourse?

Prayer
Ask God to help group members commit themselves to expressing their thoughts and feelings when developing intimate relationships.

Optional Activities
1. Ask a group member to report on the various interpretations of Song of Songs: allegorical, typical, and literal. Point out that most scholars view Song of Songs as a record of Solomon's romance with a Shulamite woman.

2. Divide into pairs and ask each person to share with his/her partner his/her views on relationships—the temptations, the heartaches, and the intimacy.

Assignment
1. Review Sessions 1–12.
2. Memorize Song of Songs 8:7.

REVIEW

Session Topic: God wants us to remember and apply what we've learned about Him from Ezra through Song of Songs. Choose one or two review methods, based on the size and interests of your group.

Option 1
Play "Stump the Panel." Ask several volunteers to participate on two panels. The remainder of the group should write questions about the Books of Ezra through Song of Songs, trying to stump the panels with their questions. If one panel is unable to answer a question, the question is passed to their opponents. Keep score to make this competitive.

Option 2
Use the names and places found in each chapter to play "Wheel of Fortune" or "Probe" with your group. New group members or members who missed several sessions will be able to participate since they merely have to choose consonants to fill in the blanks on a chalkboard or poster board. Be sure to alert each team whether the words are people, places, things, or phrases.

Option 3
Review by providing group members with the opportunity to raise questions, discuss problems, or share opinions on issues that had to be omitted during the course.

Option 4
Review the key verses from each session. Provide some sort of reward or certificate for all group members who have memorized all key verses.

Option 5
Ask: **How has this study affected your spiritual life? How has God worked in your life during this study? What did you find most helpful? Why?** Close with prayer, asking God to continue working in the spiritual, moral, and social areas of each person's life.

WRAP-UP

BibleLog Old Testament Book 3

Please take a minute to fill out and mail this form giving us your candid reaction to this material. Thanks for your help!

1. In what setting did you use this **BibleLog** study?

If you used Book 3 for personal study only, skip to question 7.
2. How many people were in your group?

3. What was the age-range of those in your group?

4. How many weeks did you spend on this study?

5. How long was your average meeting time?

6. Did you complete the studies before discussing them with a group?

7. How long did it take you to complete the study on your own?

8. Do you plan to continue the **BibleLog Series**? Why or why not?

Would you like more information on Bible study resources for small groups?

Name _____

Address _____

Church _____

City_____State_____Zip_____

PLACE
STAMP
HERE

Adult Education Editor
Victor Books
1825 College Avenue
Wheaton, Illinois 60187